REGULATIONS

AFFECTING INTERNATIONAL BANKING OPERATIONS OF BANK AND NON-BANKS

IN
AUSTRIA
CANADA
ITALY
JAPAN
SPAIN
UNITED STATES

1981-II

ORGANISATION FOR ECONOMIC CO-OPERATION AND DEVELOPMENT

The Organisation for Economic Co-operation and Development (OECD) was set up under a Convention signed in Paris on 14th December 1960, which provides that the OECD shall promote policies designed:

- to achieve the highest sustainable economic growth and employment and a rising standard of living in Member countries, while maintaining financial stability, and thus to contribute to the development of the world economy;
- to contribute to sound economic expansion in Member as well as non-member countries in the process of economic development;
- to contribute to the expansion of world trade on a multilateral, non-discriminatory basis in accordance with international obligations.

The Members of OECD are Australia, Austria, Belgium, Canada, Denmark, Finland, France, the Federal Republic of Germany, Greece, Iceland, Ireland, Italy, Japan, Luxembourg, the Netherlands, New Zealand, Norway, Portugal, Spain, Sweden, Switzerland, Turkey, the United Kingdom and the United States.

Publié en français sous le titre

RÉGLEMENTATIONS
TOUCHANT LES OPÉRATIONS BANCAIRES
INTERNATIONALES

.•.

C O N T E N T S

ALSO AVAILABLE

OECD FINANCIAL STATISTICS

This publication provides a unique collection of statistical and descriptive data on the international financial market and the national financial markets of 17 European countries, Australia, the United States, Canada and Japan.

The data are derived from more than 120 national and international sources in fourteen languages and are rendered as comparable as possible. Together with other data which have been specially compiled and are not published elsewhere, they are presented in tables which have been standardized as far as the individual features of the various financial markets permit at the present stage.

New formula as from October 1980:

Part 1. Financial Statistics Monthly

The most authoritative and the most up-to-date (2 weeks time-lag) data on the international and national financial markets:
— 350 interest rates;
— details on the Euro-bond and traditional foreign bond issues, on the medium- and long-term international bank loans and on the security issues on the domestic markets.

650 pages per year.

Part 2. Financial Accounts of OECD Countries

Flow-of-funds and balance-sheet accounts for 20 countries, detailed by sectors and by financial instruments. Integrated in an overall framework compatible with the concepts employed in the United Nations System of National Accounts.

Annual data published in 3 volumes as soon as available (750 pages per year).

Part 3. Non-financial Enterprises Financial Statement

Balance-sheets, statement of income and sources and uses of funds for a representative sample of companies in 12 countries.

Once a year (90 pages).

Methodological Supplement

Groups together the methodological notes of all the statistics reproduced in the Parts 1 to 3. These notes facilitate the interpretation of the statistics by describing their methods of calculation and the institutional context.

Once a year (200 pages).

Annual subscription to OECD Financial Statistics: F320, £35.40, US$80. Annual subscription to Financial Market Trends: F80, £8.90, US$20. Combined subscription to Financial Market Trends and to Financial Statistics Monthly: F220, £24.40, US$55.

F O R E W O R D

The papers in this volume, which is a companion to an earlier publication dealing with regulations in some other OECD countries, have been prepared in close co-operation between the OECD Secretariat and national experts, at the request of the Committee on Financial Markets. The following plan is used in each of the country notes.

Section I contains a brief exposé of the main purposes of the regulatory system of the country concerned and a sub-section with selected data on related international banking operations.

Section II describes how the regulatory system affects various types of international short- and medium-term banking transactions, distinguishing between those carried out by banks (in foreign and in domestic currency) and by non-banks to the extent that they operate with foreign banks or carry out transactions in foreign currencies also with domestic banks.

Section III contains a synoptic tabulation of regulations applied, and instruments used, by the country, classified in matrix form by balance sheet items, or by transactions, and according to categories of regulations or instruments (exchange control measures and similar devices, minimum reserve requirements, interest rate control, prudential regulations, tax regulations and other regulations and intervention instruments).

Section IV of each note expands the synoptic presentation of Section III by describing in some detail the regulations and instruments used by the country.

Section V contains a short list of references to the legal sources in whcih the regulations covered in the country notes are laid down.

Two annexes containing notes on definitions, concepts and terminology used in the country reports, and selected data on international banking showing in synoptic form the data material used for each country note, have been included in the earlier companion volume to the present publication.

AUSTRIA

I. INTRODUCTION

(i) Main purposes of the regulatory system

The Austrian monetary authorities have taken recourse to controls on international credit, loan and deposit operations for a
number of reasons. Historically, exchange market pressures have
played only a minor role in opting for capital controls. As the
Austrian foreign exchange market is very narrow, the exchange rate
is less open to external disturbances than in Germany or elsewhere.
As a matter of fact, the borrowing operations of the government and
receipts from tourism have been the major determinants of the daily
fluctuations of the external value of the Austrian schilling. Moreover, because the Austrian schilling is not traded heavily on currency
markets, the Austrian authorities were able to maintain their foreign
exchange policy even in the fact of a balance of payments deficit.

In the meantime the permanently growing interest rate elas-
ticity must be considered if foreign exchange flows are judged;
interest rate differentials - dominantly between Austria and Germany
are playing an important role and have to be eliminated in order to
pursue the foreign exchange policy. Consequently the central bank
money supply (influencing the money market rates) is practically
determined by the needs of this interest policy target. Besides,
capital imports have to be submitted to this overall objective. In
this sense, exchange controls may be considered a supplementary
instrument to the hard currency approach.

Thus, exchange controls on financial operations are maintained
mainly for the purpose of controlling domestic liquidity.

Protection of investors and depositors involved in financial
operations or, more specifically, institutional investors does not
figure prominently among the official motivations for capital controls. Rather, this is part of other regulations, particularly of
the Austrian Banking Law ("Kreditwesengesetz"). To this extent, there

7

is no need for specific prudential regulations in the exchange control system.

(ii)   Selected data on international banking operation

Over the past four years (end of 1976 to end of 1980), banks operating in Austria added heavily to their external monetary positions. Thus, foreign assets increased by 186'38 billion S, or 146 per cent to 314'47 billion S, and external liabilities rose by 226'25 billion S, or by 166 per cent to 362'37 billion S. At the end of 1980 the net external position registered a deficit of 47'90 billion S, compared to 8'02 billion S on December 31, 1976. The increase in foreign assets essentially reflects the rise in banks' loans to non-resident non-banks. Above all, the substantial expansion of loans in domestic currency to non-resident non-banks may, to a large extent, be traced back to the financing of Austrian exports via credits granted to buyers: direct credits to foreign non-banks expanded by 53'52 billion S to 77'19 billion S at the end of 1980.

When calculating the banks' external position, however, one has to take account of the banks' year-end transactions with the central bank. At the turn of 1976/77 there were year-end swaps to the extent of 7'57 billion S, at the turn of 1979/80 the volume of foreign currency operations amounted to 8'08 billion S and at the turn of 1980/81 to 8'13 billion S.

II. ANALYSIS OF REGULATIONS BY MAIN TYPES OF CAPITAL MOVEMENTS
          (situation at end-1980)

(i)   Commercial banks' foreign-currency operations

(a) External foreign-currency borrowing for relending abroad

With respect to such transactions authorised domestic banks have to apply for an individual licence, issued automatically for credits maturing within one year. In 1978 the Austrian National Bank has taken steps to limit the amount of foreign-currency credits that domestic banks may raise abroad for on-lending to foreign customers. It will approve domestic banks' foreign currency borrowings if these do not total more than the funds made available through the redemption of credits outstanding at December 31, 1978 plus 15 per cent. The following items are not subject to this ceiling on the credit-increase:
    - existing loan contracts
    - credits with a maturity over 12 months in direct connection
      with Austrian exports
    - loans to subsidiaries of Austrian trading companies and
      industrial corporations abroad as well as to joint ventures

involving equity owned by Austrian residents

- so-called transmitted credits ("Durchleiterkredite"), i.e.
tied foreign-owned funds which are transferred by domestic
banks operating in a quasi-trust relationship but in their
own name.

(b) Capital inflows via inward switching

According to the so-called "notice for employment of funds"
("Veranlagungsbescheid") authorised banks may, subject to their quota
("Manipulationsfonds") carry out specified transactions with
maturities of up to 5 years inward and outward.

(c) Capital inflows via the use of foreign-currency funds raised abroad for granting foreign-currency loans to resident non-banks

Lending in foreign currency to domestic non-banks requires
an individual licence of the Austrian National Bank. A sizeable
number of borrowers, however, have been accorded credit quotas.

(d) Capital outflows via outward switching

Within the scope of the "notice for employment of funds"
(mentioned under heading b) capital outflows via outward switching
are not subject to any restrictions.

(e) Capital outflows by way of financing external foreign-currency assets with foreign-currency deposits from resident non-banks

Foreign currency deposits with Austrian credit institutions
arising from receipts from abroad may be disposed of under general
regulations provided they are used for current payments, and under
individual licences, if they are used for capital payments.

(ii) Commercial banks' domestic currency operations with non-residents

(f) Domestic-currency liabilities to non-residents

So-called free Schilling Accounts may be freely credited with
proceeds from the sale of convertible currencies by a non-resident
to the Austrian National bank, or to an authorized bank, provided
that the conversion serves to make a "current" payment to a resident
(payments for trade purchases and services), as well as with payments
permitted by the National Bank on the basis of a general or individual
authorization. The accounts may also be freely debited (for payments
to Austrian residents from non-residents) who must, however, apply

9

for individual licences if they are to receive loans from non-residents or of the non-residents' payment serves to finance direct investment in Austria or the purchase of real estate in Austria.

(g) Placing domestic-currency-funds with foreign banks

As the Schilling is practically not used as a Euro-currency domestic-currency funds with foreign banks are of minor importance. Such transactions require an individual licence.

(h) Domestic-currency-credits and loans to non-resident non-banks

Credits, financing current payments to Austrian beneficiaries (credits extended to foreign importers of Austrian goods) are authorized on application. An individual licence is necessary for all other transactions.

(iii) Non-bank borrowing and lending operations with non-resident banks

(j) Capital inflows via borrowing from non-resident banks

As already mentioned in Section I loans and credits extended by non-residents to residents, including those in schillings from Free Schilling Accounts, at present require prior approval by the National Bank and many are restricted.

(k) Capital outflows via placing liquid assets with non-resident banks

No licences are issued to resident non-banks for capital outflows in order to create balances with foreign credit institutions.

AUSTRIA

(situation at the end of 1980)

Type of Operation or Balance Sheet Position / Type of Regulation or Instrument	Code	I. Exchange Control (1)	II. Minimum Reserve Requirements	III. Interest Rate Control	IV. Prudential Regulations	V. Tax Regulations	VI. Other Regulations or instruments
COMMERCIAL BANKS	1.						
Liability Operations/Positions	11.						
in foreign currencies	11.1						
with non-residents	11.11						
deposits from	11.111						
banks	11.111.1	X	X				
non-banks	11.111.2	X	X				
credits and loans from	11.112						
banks	11.112.1	X	X				X
non-banks	11.112.2	X	X				X
fixed-interest	11.113						X
securities							
money market paper	11.113.1	X					
bonds	11.113.2	X					
with residents	11.12						
deposits from	11.121						
banks	11.121.1						
non-banks	11.121.2		X				
Central Bank or Government	11.121.3						
in domestic currency	11.2						
with non-residents	11.21						
current accounts of	11.211						
banks	11.211.1		X				
non-banks	11.211.2		X	X			
time deposits from	11.212						
banks	11.212.1	X	X				
non-banks	11.212.2	X	X	X			
credits and loans from	11.213						
banks	11.213.1	X	X				
non-banks	11.213.2	X	X				
fixed-interest securities	11.214						
money market paper	11.214.1	X					
bonds	11.214.2	X					
Asset Operations/Positions	12.						
in foreign currencies	12.1						
with non-residents	12.11						
banks	12.111						
current accounts	12.111.1	X					
time deposits	12.111.2	X					
credits and loans	12.111.3	X					X
non-banks	12.112						
credits and loans	12.112.1	X					X
securities	12.113	X					
with residents	12.12						
deposits with banks	12.121	X					
credits and loans to non-banks	12.122	X					
securities	12.123	X					
deposits with Central bank	12.124	X					

(1) And similar regulations imposing quantitative controls on capital transactions
with non-residents.

AUSTRIA

(Contd.)   (situation at the end of 1980)

Type of Operation or Balance Sheet Position / Type of Regulation or Instrument	Code	I. Exchange Control (1)	II. Minimum Reserve Requirements	III. Interest Rate Control	IV. Prudential Regulations	V. Tax Regulations	VI. Other Regulations or instruments
in domestic currency	12.2						
with non-residents	12.21						
deposits with banks	12.211	X					
credits and loans to	12.212						
banks	12.212.1						
non-banks	12.212.2	X					
securities	12.213						
Net Positions	13.						
in foreign currencies	13.1						
vis-à-vis non-residents	13.2						
NON-BANKS	2.						
Liability Operations/Positions	21.						
credits and loans from	21.1						
non-resident banks	21.11						
in foreign currencies	21.111	X					
in domestic currency	21.112	X					
resident banks	21.12						
in foreign currencies	21.121						
Asset Operations/Positions	22.						
with non-resident banks	22.1						
in foreign currencies	22.11						
current accounts	22.111	X					
time deposits	22.112	X					
in domestic currency	22.12						
deposits	22.121	X					
with resident banks	22.2						
in foreign currencies	22.21						
current accounts	22.211						
time deposits	22.212						
FOREIGN EXCHANGE OPERATIONS/POSITIONS	3.						
Commercial Banks	31.						
spot foreign exchange dealings	31.1	X					
forward foreign exchange dealings	31.2	X					
swap transactions	31.3	X					
net foreign exchange positions	31.4						
Non-Banks	32.						
spot foreign exchange dealings	32.1	X					
forward foreign exchange dealings	32.2	X					
swap transactions	32.3	X					

(1) And similar regulations imposing quantitative controls on capital transactions with
non-residents.

IV. LISTING OF REGULATIONS BY CATEGORIES AND BY
OPERATIONS OR BALANCE SHEET POSITIONS

(situation at the end of 1980)

Code No. of classifica- tion schema	Operation/Position	Regulation

I. EXCHANGE CONTROL

I/11.111.1 I/11.111.2 I/11.112.1 I/11.112.2 I/11.113.1 I/11.113.2 I/11.111/1-3 I/12.112.1 I/12.113 I/12.121 I/12.122 I/12.123 I/12.124	Inward and outward foreign-exchange trans- actions with maturities of up to five years	Within the scope of the quota (the so-called "Manipulations- foncs") domestic credit insti- tutions may carry out such transactions. The size of this quota is determined by the Austrian National Bank in relation to the individual banks' volume of transactions.
I/11.212.1 I/11.212.2 I/11.213.1 I/11.213.2 I/11.214.1 I/11.214.2	Commercial banks' domestic-Currency operations with non- residents	see II(ii) f
I/12.211	Placing domestic- currency-funds with foreign banks	Such transactions require an individual licence.
I/12.212.2	Domestic-currency- credits and loans to non-resident non- banks	Individual licences are neces- sary for credits not financing current payments to Austrian beneficiaries.
I/21.111 I/21.112 I/22.111 I/22.112 I/22.121	Non-bank borrowing and lending operations with non-resident banks	Non-bank borrowing and lending operations with non resident banks require prior approval from the National Bank. No licences are issued to resident non-banks for capital outflows in order to create balances with foreign credit institutions.
I/31/1 I/31/2 I/31/3	Spot and forward foreign exchange operations and positions of commercial banks and swap trans- actions	These operations are not subject to any specific licencing requirements if the foreign cur- rency is sold or purchased in accordance with the regulations in force, i.e. on the basis of a general or an individual licence where required.

13

Code No. of classi- fication Schema	Operation/ Position	Regulation
I/32/1 I/32/2 I/32/3	Spot and forward foreign exchange operations and positions of resident non-banks and swap transactions	The transactions between domes- tic non-banks and domestic banks are generally authorised according to the regulations in force pertaining to the payments concerned.

II. MINIMUM RESERVE REQUIREMENTS

II/11.111 II/11.112 II/11.121.2 II/11.211 II/11.212 II/11.213	Commercial banks' liabilities to non- residents and residents in foreign currency and to non-resident non-banks in domestic currency (ex- cluding liabilities in the form of security issues)	According to the National Bank Law, minimum reserves may be required on foreign liabilities. This provision is presently (end of 1980) not applied.

III. INTEREST RATE CONTROL

III/11.211.2 III/11.212.2	Commercial banks accepting domestic currency deposits from non-resident non-banks	The Agreement on Interest Rates on Deposits (Habenzinsabkommen) has been abolished with the beginning of July 1980. The Agreement on Saving Deposits (with lawful period of notice - Eckzinsabkommen), determining a rate of 5 %, is still in force.

VI. OTHER REGULATIONS AND INSTRUMENTS

VI/12.111.3 VI/12.112.1 in combi- nation with VI.11.112.1 VI.11.112.2 VI.11.113	Commercial banks granting foreign-currency loans and credits to non-residents on the basis of funds borrowed abroad	Agreement of the OeNB with the banks on restraining the growth of foreign currency credits refinanced abroad to non- residents-

CANADA

I. INTRODUCTION

(i)   Main features of the regulatory system

The Canadian economy is highly resource and trade orientated and historically has relied heavily on foreign capital for its development. Despite high levels of domestic savings and a well developed capital market, Canada still remains a net importer of capital reflecting even higher investment levels. The Canadian authorities have generally avoided measures to inhibit the freedom of capital movements both in and out of the country. This reluctance to contemplate controls over capital movements has reflected the close interconnectness of Canada and the United States, recognition of the contribution that efficient capital markets play in the allocation of resources, and the difficulties of making controls effective.

In recent years there has been an increase in activity in the Euro-Canadian dollar deposit market. Nevertheless, the information available suggests that Canadian banks' share of this business is about one quarter of the total. This is considerably less than the share that banks of other countries have in the euro-currency business in their national currency. In addition to the difference in relative importance of national banks in the overall-euro-currency market, one reason may be that, until the end of 1980, Canadian banks were legally required to maintain reserves at the Bank of Canada on their total Canadian dollar deposit liabilities whether booked in Canada or abroad. There was also a provision in the legislation governing the operations of Canadian chartered banks that required banks to maintain adequate and appropriate assets against liabilities payable in foreign currencies.

The government has recently reviewed Canadian banking legislation. The current law, which was proclaimed in December 1980, imposes a three per cent reserve requirement on all foreign currency deposits of residents of Canada with branches and offices of banks in Canada. In addition, Canadian dollar deposits of non-residents with off-shores branches and subsidiaries are not subject to reserve requirements.

15

(ii)   Selected data on international banking operations

        Although Canadian banks have long been active in euro-currency
markets, Canada has only a very minor role as a euro-market centre.
Foreign currency business, primarily in US dollars, is much more
important than activity in domestic currency though there has been
a significant growth in Canadian dollar-denominated liabilities to
non-residents in recent years.

        Between the end of 1973 and the end of 1980, the external
assets and liabilities of banks located in Canada rose from US $ 12.3
billion to US $ 35.4 billion and from US $ 12.6 billion to US $ 43.6
billion, respectively. Their market share of the total international
banking business of the Group of Ten countries plus Switzerland
declined from 4.6 per cent to 3.8 per cent on the liabilities side.

        The net external position of the Canadian banking system, which
during the largest part of the seventies tended to fluctuate between a
net export position and a net import position, in recent years has consistently been in a net import position. In domestic currency this
amounted to the equivalent of US $ 2.4 billion at the end of 1980,
roughly triple the size of its net import position at end-1973 and
reflecting the growth of external liabilities denominated in Canadian
dollars. The net export position on foreign currencies, which in
earlier years had generally tended to offset the net import position
on domestic currency, moved into sharp deficit in 1979.

        Between the end of 1973 and the end of 1977, the growth of
domestic business was more rapid than the expansion of international
banking activity. This is reflected in the banking system's balance
sheets which show that between end-1973 and end-1977, the share of
foreign business declined from 19 per cent to 16 per cent on the
asset side and from 18 per cent to 16 per cent on the liabilities
side. However, in the last two years this trend has been reversed.
At the end of 1980, the shares of foreign business reached 21 per
cent and 24 per cent, respectively.[*]

        The Canadian dollar is of only very minor importance as a
euro-currency. Data are only available on deposits booked at
foreign branches or agencies and wholly-owned subsidiaries of
Canadian banks. However it is estimated that the gross size of the
euro-Canadian dollar deposits market at the end of 1980 was about
the equivalent of U.S. $ 2.3 billion. The main centres for euro-
Canadian dollar deposits are London and the Caribbean area.

---

[*]   The ratios are derived from data published in the IMF international
       Financial Statistics on chartered banks.

16

II. ANALYSIS OF REGULATIONS BY MAIN TYPES OF

CAPITAL MOVEMENTS

(situation at the end of 1980)

(i)　Commercial banks' foreign-currency operations

(a)　External foreign-currency borrowing for relending abroad

There are at present no obstacles - either in the form of exchange controls, interest controls or taxes - to chartered banks taking foreign-currency deposits or raising foreign-currency credits abroad for re-employing these funds in various forms (money market investments, loans and credits, securities) abroad (or domestically).

(b)　Capital inflows via inward switching

Chartered banks are free to switch foreign-currency assets into domestic currency.

(c)　Capital inflows via the use of foreign currency funds raised abroad for granting foreign currency loans to resident non-banks

There are no limitations on capital inflows via banks for purposes of granting foreign-currency loans to resident non-banks.

(d)　Capital outflows via outward switching

There are no limitations on capital outflows via banks switching domestic currency into foreign-currency assets.

(e)　Capital outflows via financing foreign-currency assets with foreign currency deposits from resident non-banks

There are no obstacles to this type of capital outflow.

(ii)　Commercial banks' domestic-currency operations with non-residents

As of the end of 1980, domestic-currency liabilities to non-resident banks and non-banks were subject to the same minimum reserve requirements as domestic-currency liabilities to residents. The current legislation removes the reserve requirement from domestic currency deposits of non-residents with branches and offices of the banks outside of Canada. However, domestic currency deposits of non-residents with branches and offices of the banks in Canada are still subject to reserves.

The required cash reserve ratio is prescribed by the Bank Act. Until June 1967, it was 8 per cent of total statutory deposits, i.e., Canadian dollar sight and time deposits. For the next eight

17

months, the required minimum monthly average on demand deposits was increased by one half of one per cent. Since February 1968, the required ratios have been 12 per cent for sight deposits and 4 per cent for time deposits as prescribed under the Bank Act. Effective January 1969, the chartered banks have been required to maintain this minimum cash reserve ratio on a half-monthly rather than a monthly basis. The averaging periods are now: (1) the business days up to and including the fifteenth of the month; and (2) all the other business days of the month.

Beginning in February 1981, the 12 per cent ratio will be gradually lowered to 10 per cent. This will be achieved by a decline of ¼ per cent every 6 months beginning March 1, 1981 and continuing until a level of 10 per cent is reached on September 1, 1984. The 4 per cent ratio on time deposits will be replaced by a ratio of 2 per cent on the first $ 500 million of time deposits, and a ratio of 3 per cent on time deposits in excess of that. The 2 per cent ratio on time deposits less than $ 500 million will become effective on February 1, 1981. On the time deposits in excess of $ 500 million, the 4 per cent ratio will be reduced by 1/8 per cent every 6 months commencing March 1, 1981 and continuing until 3 per cent is achieved on September 1, 1984.

There is now a 3 per cent reserve ratio on all foreign currency deposits of Canadian residents with branches and offices of banks in Canada. Previously, banks were required to maintain "adequate" assets against such liabilities. The 3 per cent ratio became effective February 1, 1981.

For purpose of maintaining reserves, deposit liabilities do not include deposits held under registered retirement savings plans, home ownership savings plans and retirement incomes funds as defined in Section 146 of the Income Tax Act; deposits from other banks; non-interest bearing sight deposits from members of the Canadian Payments Associations (near-banks) that are other than banks; Canadian currency deposits of non-residents with branches of the bank or its subsidiaries outside Canada. It has also been agreed to consider the removal of reserve requirements on term (time) deposits which are not encashable within one year, after passage of the proposed revisions to the Trust and Loan Company legislation. Bank debentures continue not to be regarded as deposit liabilities and are now defined in Section 132 of the Bank Act.

The Bank of Canada is empowered under Section 18(2) of the 1967 revision of the Bank of Canada Act to establish a secondary ratio

18

requirement within the range of 0 per cent to 12 per cent of
Canadian dollar deposit liabilities. The requirement was introduced
in March 1968 replacing a voluntary agreement under which the chartered banks had maintained secondary reserves equal to 7 per cent of
their Canadian dollar deposit liabilities. The chartered banks are
required to maintain this minimum secondary reserve ratio on a monthly
basis. The current requirement is 5 per cent.

Cash reserves must be held in the form of notes and non-interest
bearing deposits at the Bank of Canada. Secondary reserves comprise
interest bearing treasury bills and day-to-day loans plus any cash
reserves that are in excess of the minimum requirement.

(g) Placing domestic-currency credits and loans to non-
    resident non-banks
There are no obstacles to this type of capital outflow.

(h) Domestic-currency credits and loans to non-resident
    non-banks
There are no obstacles to this type of capital outflow.

(iii) Non-bank borrowing and lending operations with non-residents
      banks
Non-bank financial institutions in Canada are incorporated
under either federal or provincial legislation. In general, federally
incorporated financial institutions are limited to the amount of
foreign securities they may hold through the provisions of the
relevant acts governing their operations. The securities of non-
resident banks are not treated any differently than any other foreign
securities. Foreign securities must meet the same eligibility tests
as domestic securities. Many Canadian non-bank financial institutions
are permitted to invest up to 7 per cent of the book value of
guaranteed funds under a "basket" clause; foreign securities, not
otherwise eligible, may be placed in the "basket" provided the total
investment in foreign securities, "basket" and "non-basket" does not
exceed the overall foreign limitation. The federal Trust and Mortgage
Loan legislation is currently under review.

Eligible investments for provincially incorporated companies
generally correspond to federal legislation.

III. SUMMARY VIEW OF REGULATIONS AND INSTRUMENTS AFFECTING INTERNATIONAL BANKING OPERATIONS OF BANKS AND NON-BANKS IN

CANADA

(situation at the end of 1980)

Type of Operation or Balance Sheet Position / Type of Regulation or Instrument	Code	I. Exchange Control (1)	II. Minimum Reserve Requirements	III. Interest Rate Control	IV. Prudential Regulations	V. Tax Regulations	VI. Other Regulations or instruments
COMMERCIAL BANKS	1.						
Liability Operations/Positions	11.						
in foreign currencies	11.1						
with non-residents	11.11						
deposits from	11.111						
banks	11.111.1						
non-banks	11.111.2						
credits and loans from	11.112						
banks	11.112.1						
non-banks	11.112.2						
fixed-interest securities	11.113						
money market paper	11.113.1						
bonds	11.113.2						
with residents	11.12						
deposits from	11.121						
banks	11.121.1						
non-banks	11.121.2						
Central Bank or Government	11.121.3						
in domestic currency	11.2						
with non-residents	11.21						
current accounts of	11.211	X					
banks	11.211.1						
non-banks	11.211.2						
time deposits from	11.212	X				X	
banks	11.212.1						
non-banks	11.212.2						
credits and loans from	11.213					X	
banks	11.213.1						
non-banks	11.213.2						
fixed-interest securities	11.214						
money market paper	11.214.1					X	
bonds	11.214.2						
Asset Operations/Positions	12.						
in foreign currencies	12.1						
with non-residents	12.11						
banks	12.111						
current accounts	12.111.1						
time deposits	12.111.2						
credits and loans	12.111.3						
non-banks	12.112						
credits and loans	12.112.1						
securities	12.113						
with residents	12.12						
deposits with banks	12.121						
credits and loans to non-banks	12.122						
securities	12.123						
deposits with Central bank	12.124						

(1) And similar regulations imposing quantitative controls on capital transactions with non-residents.

Type of Operation or Balance Sheet Position / Type of Regulation or Instrument	Code	I. Exchange Control (1)	II. Minimum Reserve Requirements	III. Interest Rate Control	IV. Pruden-tial Regula-tions	V. Tax Regula-tions	VI. Other Regula-tions or instru-ments
in domestic currency	12.2						
with non-residents	12.21						
deposits with banks	12.211						
credits and loans to	12.212						
banks	12.212.1						
non-banks	12.212.2						
securities	12.213						
Net Positions	13.						
in foreign currencies	13.1						
vis-à-vis non-residents	13.2						
NON-BANKS	2.						
Liability Operations/ Positions	21.						
credits and loans from	21.1						
non-resident banks	21.11						
in foreign currencies	21.111					X	
in domestic currency	21.112					X	
resident banks	21.12						
in foreign currencies	21.121						
Asset Operations/Positions	22.						
with non-resident banks	22.1						
in foreign currencies	22.11						
current accounts	22.111						
time deposits	22.112						
in domestic currency	22.12						
deposits	22.121						
with resident banks	22.2						
in foreign currencies	22.21						
current accounts	22.211						
time deposits	22.212						
FOREIGN EXCHANGE OPERATIONS/ POSITIONS	3.						
Commercial Banks	31.						
spot foreign exchange dealings	31.1						
forward foreign exchange dealings	31.2						
swap transactions	31.3						
net foreign exchange positions	31.4						
Non-Banks	32.						
spot foreign exchange dealings	32.1						
forward foreign exchange dealings	32.2						
swap transactions	32.3						

(1) And similar regulations imposing quantitative controls on capital transactions with non-residents.

(situation at the end of 1980)

Code No. of classification schema	Operation/Position	Regulation

II. MINIMUM RESERVE REQUIREMENTS

II/II.211
II/II.212

Chartered banks taking sight and time deposits in domestic currency from non-resident banks and non-banks

Subject to cash reserve requirement in the form of notes and non-interest bearing deposits with Bank of Canada. Rates in effect at the end of 1980: 12 percent on sight deposits; 4 percent on time deposits.

As of February 1, 1981, the 12 percent ratio is gradually being lowered to 10 percent. The 4 percent ratio is being replaced by a 2 percent ratio on the first $500 million of time deposits and 3 percent in excess of that. The 2 percent ratio became effective February 1, 1981, and the 4 percent ratio is gradually being reduced to 3 percent.

For purposes of maintaining reserves, deposit liabilities do not include deposits held under registered retirement savings plans and retirement income funds as defined in Section 146 of the Income Tax Act; deposits from other banks; non-interest bearing sight deposits from members of the Canadian Payments Associations (near-banks that are other than banks; Canadian currency deposits of non-residents with branches of the bank or its subsidiaries outside Canada.

Code No. of classification schema	Operation/Position	Regulation
		Subject to secondary reserve requirements which comprise holdings of Treasury bills and day-to-day loans to investment dealers plus any cash reserves that are in excess of minimum requirement. The current requirement is 5 percent.

V. TAX REGULATIONS

V/II.212) V/II.213) V/II.214.1) V/21.112)	Interest payments on banks' and non-banks' liabilities to non-residents in domestic currency.	The Income Tax Act provides for a withholding tax of 25% on interest (subject to certain exemptions paid by a Canadian resident to any non-resident). This rate is reduced to 15% on payments to residents of most countries which have entered into tax treaties with Canada.
V/21.111)	Interest payments on non-banks' liabilities to non-residents in foreign currency.	Only banks chartered under the Bank Act are exempted from withholding tax on interest paid to any non-resident on deposits not repayable in Canadian currency.

MEMORANDUM ITEM:

Transactions with non-residents in fixed-interest securities in domestic currency.

Chartered banks may issue debentures under Section 72(5) of the Bank Act. For purposes of reserve requirements, bank debentures are not deposit liabilities. All corporations, including banks, may issue long-term (i.e. greater than 5 years) securities and these instruments are not subject to non-resident withholding tax.

V. PRINCIPAL SOURCES OF LEGAL AND

REGULATORY PROVISIONS

Reserve Requirements

Bank Act   1966-67 c. 87, S.1
Bank Act   1980-81 c. 40

Tax Regulations

Income Tax Act   Section 112

ITALY

I. INTRODUCTION

(1)   Main purposes of the regulatory system

During the past decade, the liberalization of capital movements, in which such headway had been made in the early sixties, has suffered a setback. Balance of payments difficulties, due initially to capital movements and subsequently to adverse trends on the current account, have led to the adoption of a series of exchange restrictions that sometimes were of a considerable severity. Among the principal administrative measures decided during this period have been the inconvertibility of Italian bank notes, limits on advanced or deferred payment of imports and exports, the ephemeral creation of a two-tier exchange market, and the requirement to set up a non interest-bearing deposit against transfers of capital and, even if for short periods, against imports of goods.

At present (end 1980) capital movements are subject to a fairly rigid set of rules. As far as commercial banks are concerned, they must balance their overall foreign exchange position daily on a currency area basis, must observe a ceiling on forward operations against lire, may not have a net external creditor position and may not grant foreign banks credits in lire in the form of overdrafts and advances. As far as non-bank residents are concerned, they may not possess purely financial short-term assets denominated in foreign currencies and may only acquire such medium and long-term assets subject to the opening of a non interest-bearing deposit of 50 per cent of their value. Direct investments, credits directly or indirectly linked to imports and exports and borrowing abroad excepted, all other types of capital transfers have either practically vanished from Italy's balance of payments (bank note remittances) or become only marginally important (portfolio investments).

Overall, the legal and administrative regulations, and exchange controls in general, adopted during the seventies for balance-of-payments reasons have produced a situation in which nearly all financial and banking transactions freely undertaken between residents and non-residents fall under the category of export and import financing.

Faced with the problem of financing balance-of-payments deficits the authorities have selected to promote inflows of capital, particular in the form of short-term bank borrowing and long-term foreign loans. These inflows are subject to control, however, for the purpose of regulating the country's overall indebtedness and the maturity structure of repayment commitments, on the one hand, and domestic liquidity on the other. The main object of the controls on the foreign exchange position of commercial banks, on the expansion of lending in domestic currency to non-residents and, in turn, on forward foreign exchange market transactions is to combat specualative attacks on the lira.

(2)   Some figures on international banking operations

Throughout the sixties and early seventies the international business of Italian banks expanded considerably. Between end-1970 and end-1973, total external assets and liabilities of domestic banks rose from US $ 9.7 billion to US $ 24.6 billion and from US $ 10.0 billion to $ 25.7 billion, respectively. In the following year, however, total external assets and liabilities declined to US $ 13.1 billion and US $ 14.9 billion, respectively at the end of 1974, partly in connection with the severe deterioration of Italy's balance of payments and with some disturbances which occurred in the euromarket, although since they have risen again to around US $ 30.7 billion and US $ 46.5 billion at end 1980.

The net external debtor position of Italian banks has been steadily increasing over the period in question and especially since 1976, when it became compulsory for resident exporters to finance short-term trade credits in foreign currency with the commercial banks. To meet the demand of resident customers, which has increased far more than stated by the administrative regulations, Italian banks have turned to the international market for funds. Their net debtor position now, at the end of 1980, stands at US $ 15.8 billion, almost all in foreign currencies, their lira net debtor position being US $ 1.9 billion. The lira, in fact, plays only a minor role on the euromarket partly because of the administrative restrictions in force at present, and non-resident residents' lira liabilities with Italian banks amounted to the equivalent of US $ 2.9 billion at end 1980.

The Italian banks' share in total euromarket assets and liabilities has fallen from 10 per cent in the period 1970-1972 to 3.5 per cent in 1975 and to 1.8 per cent (assets) and 2.8 per cent (liabilities) at the end of June 1980. This tendency has been offset, however by the expansion in intermediation abroad via branch offices, which has increased substantially in the second half of the past decade, with total assets of such branch offices amounting to US $ 16 billion at the end of 1979 or about 33 per cent of total consolidated external assets of Italian banks.

II. ANALYSIS OF REGULATIONS BY TYPES
OF CAPITAL MOVEMENTS

(situation at the end of 1930)

(1) Banks' foreign currency operations

(a) External foreign currency borrowing for relending abroad

As regards exchange controls, there are no restrictions on the raising of foreign currency funds for re-employment with non-resident banks. Operations with a maturity over 1 year, however, must be authorised by the Italian Exchange Office (IEO).

(b) Capital inflows via inward switching

It is permitted to switch foreign currency assets into lire, only on condition that the requirement to balance foreign exchange positions is observed. Hence, ceteris paribus, switching is only possible if forward cover is obtained. Forward operations against lire are subject to a ceiling.

(c) Capital inflows via the use of foreign-currency funds raised abroad for granting foreign-currency loans to resident non banks

This type of capital transfer is permitted, and has even been compulsory in some periods. Generally, however, such operations are carried out by resident non banks that are either exporters, importers or holders of authorised foreign currency accounts. Long-term loans require authorisation, which at present is granted within given ceilings.

Foreign currency funds raised abroad must be employed to finance imports, exports and other permitted operations. For strictly domestic uses authorisation must be obtained.

(d) Capital outflows via outward switching

The same rules apply as for inward switching. Outward switching via purchases of securities is subject to the same regulations on external investment as are applied to other residents.

(e) Capital outflows via foreign currency deposits of residents

These operations are limited by the fact that banks are not allowed to have a foreign-currency creditor position. Moreover, residents may only hold foreign currency accounts for a maximum of 15 days.

(2)   Banks' lire operations with non-residents

(5) Lira deposits of non-residents

Deposits in lire of non-residents are not subject to any restrictions.

(g) Placing lira funds with foreign banks

These operations are subject to authorisation, which normally is not granted.

(h) Credits and loans in lire

Credits and loans in lire require authorisation.

(3)   Non-bank borrowing and lending operations with non-resident bank

(j) Capital inflows via borrowing from non-resident banks

This type of inflow is subject to authorisation except in the case of operations with EEC countries not exceeding the value of 250 million lire, and in the case of permanent loans (loans with a maturity over 5 years, whose aim is to establish and maintain permanent economic relationships).

(k) Capital outflows via short-term investments

Subject to authorisation.

ANALYSIS OF TAX REGULATIONS GOVERNING
INTEREST PAYMENTS

(1)   Commercial banks' operations

(a) Liabilities

Non-resident deposits, in either domestic or foreign currency, have no tax restrictions when the operations involve only non-resident banks. In fact, the interest on deposits and current-account balances from non-resident banks, including Italian banks' own branches abroad, is specifically exempted from withholding tax.

This is the only exception to the general rule that the interest on all deposits, whether of resident banks, resident non banks or non-resident non banks, in either domestic or foreign currency, is subject to a withholding tax of 20 per cent, which is paid by resident limited companies or equivalent bodies as an advance of corporate tax and by other depositors (individuals and non-resident companies and bodies) as a definitive tax.

(b) Assets

Lending in domestic or foreign currency to residents or non residents has no tax restrictions when in the form of credits and loans and the interest received is therefore exempt from withholding tax.

On the other hand, the interest on deposits with non-resident banks or on foreign fixed-interest securities is subject to a withholding tax of 15 and 30 per cent respectively, with the exception of securities issued by international organisations which enjoy a special tax treatment. However, on interest not paid out by resident intermediaries but collected or credited to an account abroad, no withholding tax is levied.

Foreign currency deposits with Italian banks or foreign currency securities issued by residents are subject to the same tax provisions (securities: exemption or withholding tax of 10 or 20 per cent; deposits: withholding tax of 20 per cent) as domestic currency deposits or securities.

Lastly, interest received on securities issued abroad to finance export credits are exempt from withholding tax.

(2)   Non-bank borrowing and lending operations

Direct foreign currency borrowing abroad by non banks is subject to taxation: a definitive tax of 15 per cent is levied on the interest at the time of payment, except in the case of interest on funds employed for export finance, which are expressly exempted from taxation.

On the other hand, no withholding tax is applied to the interest on credit or loans granted by a foreign branch of a resident bank, or to that on foreign currency borrowing with resident banks.

Interest on foreign-currency deposits and claims with non-resident banks are subject to a 15 per cent withholding tax, which is not applied, however, if the interest is collected or credited abroad. On the other hand, the interest on current-account balances and deposits in foreign currency with resident banks is subject to a withholding tax of 20 per cent, as are all domestic-currency deposits.

The withholding tax represents an advance of corporate tax for limited companies or equivalent bodies and a definitive tax for other depositors.

ITALY
(situation at the end of 1980)

Type of Operation or Balance Sheet Position \ Type of Regulation or Instrument	Code	I. Exchange Control (1)	II. Minimum Reserve Requirements	III. Interest Rate Control	IV. Prudential Regulations	V. Tax Regulations	VI. Other Regulations or instruments
COMMERCIAL BANKS	1.						
Liability Operations/Positions	11.						
in foreign currencies	11.1				X		
with non-residents	11.11						
deposits from	11.111	X					
banks	11.111.1						
non-banks	11.111.2					X	
credits and loans from	11.112						
banks	11.112.1	X					
non-banks	11.112.2	X				X	
fixed-interest	11.113	X					
securities							
money market paper	11.113.1						
bonds	11.113.2						
with residents	11.12						
deposits from	11.121						
banks	11.121.1					X	
non-banks	11.121.2	X				X	
Central Bank or Government	11.121.3						
in domestic currency	11.2						
with non-residents	11.21						
current accounts of	11.211						
banks	11.211.1		X				
non-banks	11.211.2		X			X	
time deposits from	11.212						
banks	11.212.1		X				
non-banks	11.212.2		X			X	
credits and loans from	11.213	X					
banks	11.213.1		X				
non-banks	11.213.2		X				
fixed-interest securities	11.214	X					
money market paper	11.214.1						
bonds	11.214.2						
Asset Operations/Positions	12.						
in foreign currencies	12.1						
with non-residents	12.11						
banks	12.111						
current accounts	12.111.1	X				X	
time deposits	12.111.2	X				X	
credits and loans	12.111.3	X					
non-banks	12.112						
credits and loans	12.112.1						
securities	12.113	X				X	
with residents	12.12						
deposits with banks	12.121					X	
credits and loans to non-banks	12.122	X					
securities	12.123	X				X	
deposits with Central bank	12.124	X					

(1) And similar regulations imposing quantitative controls on capital transactions with non-residents.

ITALY

(Contd.)

(situation at the end of 1980)

Type of Operation or Balance Sheet Position / Type of Regulation or Instrument	Code	I. Exchange Control (1)	II. Minimum Reserve Requirements	III. Interest Rate Control	IV. Prudential Regulations	V. Tax Regulations	VI. Other Regulations or instruments
in domestic currency	12.2						
with non-residents	12.21						
deposits with banks	12.211	X					
credits and loans to	12.212	X					
banks	12.212.1						
non-banks	12.212.2						
securities	12.213	X				X	
Net Positions	13.						
in foreign currencies	13.1	X					
vis-à-vis non-residents	13.2	X					
NON-BANKS	2.						
Liability Operations/ Positions	21.						
credits and loans from	21.1	X					
non-resident banks	21.11						
in foreign currencies	21.111					X	
in domestic currency	21.112					X	
resident banks	21.12	X					
in foreign currencies	21.121						
Asset Operations/Positions	22.						
with non-resident banks	22.1	X					
in foreign currencies	22.11						
current accounts	22.111					X	
time deposits	22.112					X	
in domestic currency	22.12	X					
deposits	22.121						
with resident banks	22.2	X					
in foreign currencies	22.21						
current accounts	22.211					X	
time deposits	22.212					X	
FOREIGN EXCHANGE OPERATIONS/ POSITIONS	3.						
Commercial Banks	31.						
spot foreign exchange dealings	31.1	X					
forward foreign exchange dealings	31.2	X					
swap transactions	31.3	X					
net foreign exchange positions	31.4						
Non-Banks	32.						
spot foreign exchange dealings	32.1	X					
forward foreign exchange dealings	32.2	X					
swap transactions	32.3	X					

(1) And similar regulations imposing quantitative controls on capital transactions with non-residents.

(situation at the end of 1980)

CODE	OPERATION/POSITION	REGULATION
	Commercial Banks	
I/11.111	Foreign currency time deposits from non residents with maturity over one year	Subject to authorisation by the Italian Exchange Office
I/11.112.1	Foreign currency credits and loans granted by non-resident banks	Subject to prior authorisation: a) by Ministry of Foreign Trade or by IEO for maturities over 180 days (proceeds to be used to finance commercial or financial operations permitted by exchange regulations) b) by Ministry of the Treasury and Ministry of Foreign Trade, irrespective of maturity, if proceeds of loans are to be switched into lire to finance claims on residents.
I/11.112.2	Foreign-currency credits and loans granted by non-resident non banks	Subject to prior authorisation by the Ministry of Foreign Trade and the Ministry of the Treasury jointly. These transactions have to no practical importance
I/11.113.	Commercial banks' issues of short and long-term fixed-interest securities in foreign currencies to non residents	See 11.112.2 above
I/11.121.2	Foreign-currency deposits from resident non banks	Permitted for foreign currencies quoted in the Italian foreign exchange market acquired through or to be used for external transactions. Normally such deposits can only be held for a maximum of 15 days. Certain categories of operators are eligible to hold current accounts that are not subject to closure after 15 days (authorised accounts).
I/11.213	Credits and loans in domestic currency granted by non-resident banks and non-banks, excluding advances, with a minimum maturity of six months, for the financing of commercial or financial transactions	Subject to authorisation: a) by Ministry of Foreign Trade for advances with a maturity over six months b) by Ministry of Foreign Trade and Ministry of Treasury jointly for other loans (these operations have no practical importance)
I/11.214	Issues of short and long-term fixed interest securities in domestic currency to non residents	See 11.112.2

32

CODE	OPERATION/POSITION	REGULATION
I/12.111.2	Foreign currency time deposits with non-resident banks, with a maturity over one year	Subject to authorisation by IEO
I/12.111.1) 12.111.3)	Credits and loans to non-residents, other than advances, with a maximum maturity of six months, predominantly to finance commercial transactions	Subject to authorisation by Ministry of Foreign Trade
I.12.113	a) Purchase of unlisted securities in foreign currencies b) Purchases of listed securities in foreign currencies excluding those financed via increases in foreign-currency liabilities	Subject to the regulations governing investments abroad (direct and portfolio). Specifically, investments of this type, with a few exceptions, are subject to the establishment of a non-interest bearing deposit in line with the same maturity as the investments and for an amount equal to 50 per cent of their value. Exemption from the deposit requirement is normally granted in the case of direct investments, sometimes combined with a requirement to finance the investment by increasing foreign currency liabilities abroad
I.12.122	Loans and advances in foreign currencies to resident non banks not falling into the following main categories: - short-term "supplier credits" (original maturity not over six months) - advances to importers and holders of "authorised accounts" as above (11.121.2) with original maturity not over six months	Subject to authorisation by Ministry of Foreign Trade, which is normally granted
I.12.123	Purchases of foreign currency securities issued by residents other than those financed by increasing foreign currency liabilities (cf. 12.113)	Subject to the regulations governing portfolio investments (deposit of 50 per cent of value in non-interest bearing account as under 12.113 above)
I.12.124	Foreign currency deposits with IEO	Only on the initiative of IEO
I.12.211	Lira deposits with non-resident banks	Virtually prohibited
I.12.212	Short- and long-term loans and advances in lire granted to non residents	Subject to authorisation by the Ministry of Foreign Trade

CODE	OPERATION/POSITION	REGULATION
I.12.213	a) Securities in lire issued in Italy by non residents	a) No restrictions
	b) Securities in lire issued abroad by non residents	b) Subject to the regulations governing portfolio investments (cf. 12.123 above)
I.13.1	Net spot and forward foreign exchange position	As a rule banks must balance their global forward and spot foreign exchange position on a daily basis and separately for each of the following currencies or groups of currencies: a) dollar b) EEC currencies together c) other currencies together
I.13.2	Net foreign position	Creditor position prohibited
	Non-banks	
I.21.1	a) Credits and loans granted by banks resident outside EEC, irrespective of maturity and amount	Subject to joint authorisation by Ministry of Foreign Trade and Ministry of the Treasury
	b) Credits and loans granted by banks resident in EEC, with a maturity over five years and for an amount over 250 million lire	
I.21.12	Cf. 12.122	Cf. 12.122
I.22.1	Foreign currency deposits and current accounts with non-resident banks	Subject to authorisation by Ministry of Foreign Trade
I.22.12	Lira deposits with non-resident banks	As a general rule, prohibited
I.22.2	Foreign currency deposits and current accounts with resident banks	Cf. 11.121.2

FOREIGN EXCHANGE OPERATIONS

I.31.1 31.2	Foreign Exchange Operations: Spot and forward foreign exchange transactions by resident banks	No restriction, within the limits established for the net position (13.1) and by the regulations governing transactions with non banks, i.e.: a) resident banks may only sell foreign exchange forward to non resident non banks to cover exchange risks connected with finance granted to the same non resident non banks b) forward operations with residen non banks are limited to those specified under 32.2 below

CODE	OPERATION/POSITION	REGULATION
I.31.3	Spot purchases (sales) by commercial banks of foreign currencies against lire, combined with forward sales (purchases) of foreign currencies against lire	Net forward sales (purchases) of lire are subject to a ceiling fixed separately for each bank. Transactions of this type can only be carried out with resident and non-resident banks
I.32.1	Spot foreign exchange transactions by resident non banks	Permitted only with Italian banks in the case of operations allowed under exchange regulations
I.32.2	Outright forward foreign exchange transactions by resident non banks	Permitted only with Italian banks to cover exchange risks connected with commercial transactions and authorised financing operations (cf. 12.122 above)
I.32.3	Swap transactions by resident non banks	Prohibited

II. MINIMUM RESERVE REQUIREMENTS

II.11.211	Non residents' lira liabilities, irrespective of origin	Since 1st February 1975, commercial banks must set up each month a compulsory reserve with the Bank of Italy amounting to 15.75 per cent of the increase in total deposits, excluding contemporaneous increases in capital and reserves. Total deposits consist of the following items:

a) savings deposits

b) current accounts of ordinary customers

c) deposits and current accounts of special credit institutions

d) all lira funds of non residents, whatever their origin

IV. PRUDENTIAL REGULATIONS

IV.11.1	Foreign currency liabilities, except short-term	The Italian system makes a distinction between short-term credit operations and medium- and long-term operations, the first being conducted as a rule by the commercial banks, the second being the preserve of the special credit institutions.

The concept of separation has, however, evolved over the years. On the one hand, the criterion of rigid separation between short and medium and long-term credit operations has been criticised and been replaced by what is known as functional specialisation, i.e. the special credit institutions are responsible for the financing of investment, even when short-term lending is involved as in the case of prefinancing. In

IV.11.1 contd.

addition, since it was not felt to be incompatible with the principles of the Italian system to permit commercial banks to extend their operations beyond the short term, particularly in the case of finance for exports and operations not linked to specific investment programmes generally, the Supervisory Authorities issued a series of instructions during the seventi which have increased the commercial banks' freedom to carry ou operations exceeding the short term. Specifically, in the cas of foreign currency liabilities and assets exceeding the short term, the regulations state tha the Bank of Italy, at the reque of the individual credit instit tion, may:

1) establish a ceiling, includi a revolving ceiling, on foreign currency borrowing and deposits with a maturity over 18 months but generally not exceeding five years. T investment of these funds mu comply with the following conditions:

   a) the rate of interest on finance granted must be reviewed at least every s months if the borrowed fu carry variable interest rates;

   b) the global credit with a maturity over 18 months deriving from lending ope tions, calculated on the basis of the residual lif of the operations and not the residual life accordi to the original contracts may not exceed total borrowed funds with a res dual life over 18 months;

   c) the average residual life of the above lending oper tions may not exceed by more than six months the average residual life of the corresponding assets

2) establish operating ceilings in absolute amounts or as a percentage of short-term foreign-currency assets, on foreign currency transaction exceeding the short-term by authorised foreign exchange dealers, in addition to the limits specified above.

CODE	OPERATION/POSITION	REGULATION

V. TAX REGULATIONS

Commercial banks

V.11.111.2	Foreign currency banks deposits from non-resident non banks	Interest subject to 20 per cent definitive withholding tax, unless more favourable treatment is provided for under international conventions to prevent double taxation
V.11.112.2	Foreign currency credits and loans granted by non-resident non banks	Interest subject to 15 per cent definitive withholding tax, unless more favourable treatment is provided for under international conventions to prevent double taxation
V.11.121.1	Foreign-currency deposits from resident banks	Interest subject to 20 per cent withholding tax as an advance of tax due by depositor
V.11.121.2	Foreign-currency deposits from resident non banks	Interest subject to 20 per cent withholding tax, definitively, or as an advance of corporate tax, depending on the type of the depositors. Interest
V.11.211.2 11.212.2	Current account balances and time deposits in domestic currency from non-resident non banks	Interest subject to 20 per cent definitive withholding tax
V.12.111.1 12.111.2	Foreign currency current account balances and time deposits with non-resident banks	Interest on both types of account subject to 15 per cent withholding tax as an advance of corporate tax due by bank, but only if paid by resident intermediaries; if interest is credited to an account abroad, no withholding tax is levied.
V.12.113	Fixed-interest securities in foreign currency issued by non-resident non banks	Interest subject to 30 per cent withholding tax as an advance of corporate tax due by bank, when the securities have been deposited in special accounts with banks in Italy, after 1.1.1974; if deposited in such accounts before 1.1.1974 no withholding tax is levied on the interest
V.12.121	Deposits in foreign currencies with resident banks	Interest subject to 20 per cent withholding tax as an advance of corporate tax due by banks
V.12.123	Securities in foreign currencies issued by residents	Interest subject to no withholding tax or subject to withholding tax of 10 or 20 per cent depending on issuer and time of subscription:

1) Withholding tax is levied:

    a) at the rate of 10 per cent on interest on securities issued by medium and long-term credit institutions

b) at the rate of 20 per cent
on interest on securities
issued by private companie
unless more favourable
treatment is provided for
under conventions to preve
vent double taxation

2) Withholding tax is not levied
on:

a) interest on securities,
irrespective of issuer,
subscribed before 1.1.'74
and interest on public
bonds (government and certain public bodies) irrespective of date of issue

b) interest on securities
issued abroad by medium an
long-term credit institu-
tions to cover export
credit operations

c) interest on securities
issued by credit institu-
tions under a)-1) subscrib
between 3/7/80 and 30/9/80
unconditionally and betwee
1/10/80 and 30/9/80 if
maturity is over three
years and subscription not
linked to reimbursement of
previous securities

d) interest on securities by
issued by holding companie
of state-controlled cor-
porations and by listed
joint-stock companies if
maturity is over three
years and subscription not
linked to reimbursement of
previous securities
acquired between 31/12/80
and 30/3/81

CODE	OPERATION/POSITION	REGULATION
V.12.213	Securities in domestic currency issued in Italy or abroad by non-residents	Interest subject to 30 per cent withholding tax as an advance of of corporate tax due by bank; interest on securities issued by international organisations enjoying special treatment (IBRD EEC, ECEC, EURATOM) are not taxe
	Non-Banks	
V/21.111 21.112	Credits and loans by non-resident banks in foreign or domestic currency	Interest subject to 15 per cent definitive tax, unless more favourable treatment is provided for under international conven- tions to prevent double taxation Interest is not subject to with- holding tax if credit is granted by a foreign branch abroad of a resident bank, or if credits and loans are used to finance export

CODE	OPERATION/POSITION	REGULATION
V.21.111 21.112	Current-account balances and time deposits in foreign currency with non-resident banks	Interest if paid by resident intermediaries subject to 15 per cent withholding tax, as an advance of corporate tax, if depositor is a limited company or equivalent body, and definitively in other cases (cf. 12.111.1).

VI. PRINCIPAL SOURCES OF LEGAL AND REGULATORY PROVISIONS

Exchange controls

(1) Decree No. 586 of 28/7/1955. Transactions on the foreign exchange market and surrender of foreign currency to the IEO:

(2) Decree No. 476 of 6/6/1956. New exchange regulations and creation of a free market for State-issued notes and foreign bank notes.

(3) Ministerial Decree of 7/8/1978. Provisions relating to exchange regulations and financial relations with other countries.

(4) Circular issued by the Ministry of Foreign Trade "Invisible transactions and miscellaneous provisions".

(5) Italian Exchange Office pamphlet "Instructions to banks".

Minimum reserve requirement

(1) Royal Decree No. 375 of 12/3/1936 (Banking Act) Art. 32, letter f.

(2) Resolution of the Interministerial Committee for Credit and Saving of 30/1/1975 regulating the reserve requirement.

(3) Resolution of the Interministerial Committee for Credit and Saving of 4/2/1976 concerning, among other matters, the change in the percentage rate of the reserve requirement, now standing at 15.75 per cent.

(4) Instructions issued by the Bank of Italy.

Prudential regulations

(1) Resolution of the Interministerial Committee for Credit and Saving of 4/6/1976 concerning the authorisation of foreign exchange dealer banks to raise on foreign markets foreign currency funds with a maturity over the short term (18 months).

Prudential regulations (contd.)

(2) Decree of the Ministry of the Treasury of 12/8/1979 concerning amendments to the above resolution.

(3) Instructions issued by the Bank of Italy.

Tax regulations

(1) Presidential Decree No. 600 of 29/9/1973 and subsequent amendments art. 26 (normal system of withholding tax on interest).

(2) Presidential Decree No. 601 of 29/9/1973 art. 31 (Preferential treatment for public securities)

(3) Law No. 277 of 24/5/1977 and Law No. 393 of 27/7/1978 art. 4 (preferential treatment for operations relating to the financing of exports).

(4) Law No. 687 of 28/10/1980 art. 3 (Preferential treatment for securities subscribed between 3/7/1980 and 30/9/1980).

(5) Decree No. 693 of 31/10/1980 art. 6, converted into Law No. 891 of 22/12/1980 (Preferential treatment for securities subscribed between 1/10/1980 and 30/9/1981).

JAPAN

I. INTRODUCTION

(i) Main purposes of the regulatory system

The Japanese external situation has dramatically changed since the reconstruction of the economy after World War II. While the basic situation throughout the decade of the 1950s and early 1960s was one of chronic current-account deficits, the balance of payments began to improve in the mid-'60s. This trend towards rising surplus was interrupted in 1973-74 and from 1979 onwards, when the Japanese balance-of-payments situation deteriorated as a result of the first and second oil crises. Although the current account situation during the second oil crisis was worse than that of the first one, the deficit on current account has been decreasing since the summer of 1980 and recently has turned into surplus again.

It is noteworthy that consistently there has been a strong demand for foreign funds in Japan, even when the overall balance of payments turned into a surplus. One of the reasons for this phenomenon is to be found in domestic financial market conditions which caused private credit demands to spill over rather strongly into external markets. It appears that policy intentions toward more yen financing will require further liberalisation of internal Japanese markets and particularly an interest-rate structure that to a greater extent is based on market forces.

Since 1968, Japan has particularly accelerated the tempo of relaxing exchange controls to achieve substantial overall liberalisation of foreign transactions. As from December 1980, the amended Foreign Exchange and Foreign Trade Control Law (established on 1st December, 1949, amended 18th December, 1979) which is based on freedom in principle on external transactions, came into force, and liberalisation of current and capital transactions was more completely achieved. The objective of this Law is to enable proper expansion of external transactions, on the basis of freedom of foreign exchange, foreign trade, and other external transactions, with necessary but minimum control.

Provisions under the law differentiate carefully among residents and non-residents, and among banks and non-banks. In order to facilitate daily operations, especially those that are trade related, certain Japanese banks (and branches of foreign banks in Japan) are recognised as "authorised foreign exchange banks". Most of these are empowered to establish correspondence relations with banks outside Japan.

From the view-point of maintaining sound banking and of avoiding abrupt foreign exchange movement, banks are subject to special regulations, particularly a ceiling on the overall foreign exchange position which is specifically determined by the authorities for each bank.

The Ministry of Finance (MOF) is responsible for formulating general policies regarding exchange control matters and international banking activities of commercial banks. Empowered by the Ministry of Finance, the Bank of Japan (BOJ) takes charge of executing exchange control regulations.

(ii) Selected data on international banking operations

Japanese banks have played a rather modest role internationally when compared to institutions of US or European origin. While the authorities fostered the establishment of foreign branches by the Bank of Tokyo during the decade of the 1950s, these branches served primarily the purpose of promoting the efficient execution of international payments related to trade.

Towards the end of the 1960s it became clear that the changing needs of the country's economy required a strong international involvement of its banking institutions. In addition, the balance of payments situations permitted the relaxation of certain restrictions. Since that time, the international involvement of Japan's banks has been increasing significantly.

However, when related to the size of the Japanese economy and its participation in international trade, the role of the Japanese banks in international finance is still relatively small.

The financing of Japanese exports and imports, largely through advances to Japanese trading companies, represents the major business of the foreign branches ("usance financing"). Their funding is made in their respective local interbank markets or the euro-currency markets The foreign affiliates of Japanese banks have also been very active in raising funds in the euro-markets for loans to their clients ("medium- and long-term loans").

As Japanese industry began to invest abroad in productive assets at an accelerating pace beginning in the late 1960s and early 1970s, the Japanese banks found an additional and important field of activity. After an aborted attempt in 1974, the banks have, since 1976, again started to actively participate in syndicated loans to non-Japanese international borrowers, including less-developed countries through both their head offices and their branches. They were prompted by weak domestic loan demand. Towards the first half of 1981, the market share of Japanese bank's medium- and long-term loans in euro-currency bank credits was estimated at about 15 per cent.

These activities are reflected in the data. Between the end of 1973 and the end of 1980, external assets and liabilities of banks located in Japan rose from US $ 17.1 billion to US $ 65.7 billion and from US $ 13.6 billion to US $ 80.2 billion respectively. Their market share of the total international banking business of the Group of Ten countries plus Switzerland declined from 6.4 per cent at the end of 1973 to 5.7 per cent at end-1980 on the assets side; at the same time Japan's share of total liabilities amounted to 6.3 per cent at the end of 1980, against 4.7 per cent end-1973.

Tokyo's position as a euro-market centre is rather modest relative to its potential. Indeed, its role has weakened relative to the total that is comprised of BIS reporting countries, North America, the Caribbean area and the remainder of the Far East. Tokyo's share of total foreign currency deposits decreased from 8.2 per cent in 1974 to 6.4 per cent in 1980. Withholding taxes and reserve requirements make the market non-competitive for transactions involving non-residents on both sides. What does exist is a relatively small dollar call market that serves banks who can lay off dollar funds on a very short-term basis.

Since mid-1977, the quantitative ceilings for medium- and long-term loans abroad have been removed and a funding ratio was put in its place that compels Japanese banks to match on the liability side the maturity of their loan commitments. It must also be noted that the funding ratio does not apply to subsidiaries of Japanese banks abroad.

Despite Japan's chronic balance-of-payments surpluses, the Japanese banking system has turned from a net capital exporter to a net capital importer position which at the end of 1980 amounted to US $ 14.5 billion as compared with a net asset position of US $ 3.4 billion prevailing at the end of 1973. All of the turn-around in the net external position took place in the foreign-currency sector where the net external liabilities position amounted to US $ 19.2 billion at the end of 1980, as compared with the net external assets position of US $ 3.4 billion at the end of 1973, largely reflecting increased foreign-currency lending by Tokyo banks to resident firms. In domestic currency, Japanese banks had a net creditor position of $ 4.6 billion at end-1980, against near-balance at end-1973, reflecting a major expansion of yen-denominated lending

At the end of 1978, taking the Japanese city banks as a whole, foreign business accounted for 2.3 per cent at the end of 1978 on the assets side, down from 2.6 per cent at the end of 1973. However, on the liabilities side, the figure was 4.0 per cent at the end of 1978, rising from 3.6 per cent at the end of 1973 [1].

As far as external credit transactions are concerned, the Japanese yen plays an insignificant role. Considering the economic power of Japan in terms of GNP, foreign trade, and FDI, the international utilisation of the yen in international trade settlement and financing has been far lower than those of DM, sterling and Swiss francs. While a yen-section of the euro-currency market exists, it is extremely small and based almost exclusively on external dollar deposits or dollar loans covered with yen forward exchange transactions of the same maturity.

II. ANALYSIS OF REGULATIONS BY MAIN TYPES OF CAPITAL MOVEMENTS

(Situation at the end of 1980)

(i)   Commercial banks' foreign-currency operations

(a) External foreign-currency borrowing for relending aborad

Commercial banks are permitted to raise foreign currency funds from non-residents for the purpose of relending abroad.

(b) Capital inflows via inward switching

Regulations have been in existence since 1968 in order to prevent inflows of short-term foreign funds from disturbing monetary policy and foreign exchange market. The Ministry of Finance supervises these regulations on a daily basis through BOJ.

The net conversion of foreign currencies into yen by branches of foreign banks and by Japanese banks is allowed up to a certain amount. The amount is determined for each bank on the basis of some objective criteria; branches of foreign banks receive at times preferential treatment in this regard.

(c) Capital inflows via the use of foreign currency funds raised abroad for granting foreign-currency loans to resident non-banks

This type of lending is a very important activity of foreign banks and is generally known under the term "impact loan".

---

[1] The ratios mentioned are derived from data published in the IMF International Financial Statistics on Deposit Money Banks. Deposit Money Banks include commercial banks and other banks that have large demand deposits.

This loan does not require a prior notice so long as it is extended by authorised foreign exchange banks. Terms and conditions of such loans, including the interest rate, are negotiated among entities concerned; in effect, such loans are made at market rate dictated by conditions abroad.

(d) Capital outflows via outward switching

The scope for outward switching is limited, with the cost of yen funds being often prohibitive, especially when cover costs are considered.

Lending abroad on an uncovered basis is limited by restraints on the banks' overall position.

(e) Capital outflows via financing external foreign-currency deposits from resident non-banks

A resident is freely allowed to place foreign currency deposits with banks in Japan; however, this type of capital outflow is not so important, because the amount of foreign currency deposits by residents is negligible.

(ii) Commercial bank's domestic-currency operations with non residents

(f) Domestic-currency liabilities to non-residents

Non-resident Japanese-yen deposits held with banks in Japan are basically free from regulations imposed by the authorities. However, the maximum interest rates on deposits are limited except for deposits placed by foreign governments or international organisations.

(g) Placing domestic currency funds with foreign banks

There are no restrictions to this type of capital outflow.

(h) Domestic-currency loans to non-resident non banks

In principle, only prior notification is required for commercial banks to extend domestic currency loans to non-resident non banks.

(iii) Non-bank borrowing and lending operation with non-resident banks

Those transactions would only require prior notification to the authorities. Although non-bank lending operations are increasing in numbers for the recent months, non-bank borrowings of domestic currency from non-resident banks are very rarely developed.

III. SUMMARY VIEW OF REGULATIONS AND INSTRUMENTS AFFECTING INTERNATIONAL BANKING OPERATIONS OF BANKS AND NON-BANKS IN JAPAN

(situation at the end of 1980)

Type of Operation or Balance Sheet Position / Type of Regulation or Instrument	Code	I. Exchange Control (1)	II. Minimum Reserve Requirements	III. Interest Rate Control	IV. Prudential Regulations	V. Tax Regulations	VI. Other Regulations or instruments
COMMERCIAL BANKS	1.						
Liability Operations/Positions	11.						
in foreign currencies	11.1						
with non-residents	11.11					X	
deposits from	11.111		X				
banks	11.111.1					X	
non-banks	11.111.2						
credits and loans from	11.112	(2)	X				
banks	11.112.1					X	
non-banks	11.112.2						
fixed interest securities	11.113	(2)					
money market paper	11.113.1						
bonds	11.113.2						
with residents	11.12						
deposits from	11.121						
banks	11.121.1		X				
non-banks	11.121.2		X				
Central Bank or Government	11.121.3						
in domestic currency	11.2						
with non-residents	11.21					X	
current accounts of	11.211		X	X			
banks	11.211.1						
non-banks	11.211.2						
time deposits from	11.212		X	X			
banks	11.212.1						
non-banks	11.212.2						
credits and loans from	11.213	(2)					
banks	11.213.1						
non-banks	11.213.2						
fixed-interest securities	11.214	(2)	X				
money market paper	11.214.1						
bonds	11.214.2						
Asset Operations/Positions	12.						
in foreign currencies	12.1						
with non-residents	12.11						
banks	12.111						
current accounts	12.111.1						
time deposits	12.111.2						
credits and loans	12.111.3	(2)					
non-banks	12.112	(2)					
credits and loans	12.112.1						
securities	12.113	(2)					
with residents	12.12						
deposits with banks	12.121						
credits and loans to non-banks	12.122						
securities	12.123						
deposits with Central bank	12.124						

(1) And similar regulations imposing quantitative controls on capital transactions with non-residents.

(2) Subject to a prior notice, but most of these transactions by the major authorised foreign exchange banks are exempt from it.

(Contd.)

JAPAN
(situation at the end of 1980)

Type of Operation or Balance Sheet Position / Type of Regulation or Instrument	Code	I. Exchange Control (1)	II. Minimum Reserve Requirements	III. Interest Rate Control	IV. Prudential Regulations	V. Tax Regulations	VI. Other Regulations or instruments
in domestic currency	12.2						
with non-residents	12.21						
deposits with banks	12.211						
credits and loans to	12.212	(2)					
banks	12.212.1						
non-banks	12.212.2						
securities	12.213						
Net Positions	13.						
in foreign currencies	13.1	X					
vis-à-vis non-residents	13.2						
NON-BANKS	2.						
Liability Operations/ Positions	21.						
credits and loans from	21.1						
non-resident banks	21.11	(2)					
in foreign currencies	21.111						
in domestic currency	21.112						
resident banks	21.12						
in foreign currencies	21.121						
Asset Operations/Positions	22.						
with non-resident banks	22.1						
in foreign currencies	22.11	X					
current accounts	22.111						
time deposits	22.112						
in domestic currency	22.12	X					
deposits	22.121						
with resident banks	22.2						
in foreign currencies	22.21						
current accounts	22.211						
time deposits	22.212						
FOREIGN EXCHANGE OPERATIONS/ POSITIONS	3.						
Commercial Banks	31.						
spot foreign exchange dealings	31.1						
forward foreign exchange dealings	31.2						
swap transactions	31.3						
net foreign exchange positions	31.4	X					
Non-Banks	32.						
spot foreign exchange dealings	32.1	X					
forward foreign exchange dealings	32.2	X					
swap transactions	32.3	X					

(1) And similar regulations imposing quantitative controls on capital transactions with non-residents.

(2) Subject to a prior notice, but most of these transactions by the major authorised foreign exchange banks are exempt from it.

IV. LISTING OF REGULATIONS BY CATEGORIES AND BY OPERATIONS OR BALANCE SHEET POSITIONS

(Situation at the end of 1980)

Code no. of classification schema	Operation/position	Regulation
		I. EXCHANGE CONTROL
I/13.1	Net positions of commercial banks by foreign currencies	In principle, banks must match positions at all times. Daily limits are set for each bank - see 31.4
I/22.11	Non-banks holdings current accounts and time deposits with non-resident banks in foreign currencies	Limited to designated insurance, transport, securities, trading companies. These companies are granted blanket licences by BoJ. Since 1st April, 1978 individuals may hold up to Yen 3 million upon permission by BoJ.
I/22.12	Non-banks holding domestic currency deposits with non-resident banks	Individuals up to Yen 3 million upon permission by BoJ.
I/31.4	Net foreign exchange positions of commercial banks	In principle, forex positions should match. Limits given by authorities to individual authorised foreign exchange banks, enforced by daily reporting.
I/32.1 I/32.2	Spot and forward foreign exchange dealings against domestic currency by non-banks	Not permitted to enter primary market directly; must deal through authorised foreign exchange banks, who will execute transactions.
I/32.3	Swap transactions by non-banks involving domestic currency	Not permitted.
		II. MINIMUM RESERVE REQUIREMEN
II/11.111 II/11.112 II/11.121.1 II/11.121.2	Commercial banks acquiring foreign currency deposits from non-residents and residents	Subject to min. res. of 0.25 p cent. Japanese authorities do not subject foreign affiliates of Japanese banks to min. res. requirements.
II/11.211 II/11.212 II/11.214	Commercial banks acquiring domestic currency funds from non-residents in various forms	Subject to min. res. of 0.25 p 0.25 per cent.
		III. INTEREST RATE CONTROL
III/11.211 III/11.212	Commercial banks acquiring domestic currency deposits from non-residents	The maximum interest rates on deposits are limited

Code no. of classification schema	Operation/position	Regulation
		V. TAX REGULATIONS
V/11.11 V/11.21	Commercial banks acquiring funds from non-residents	Income tax at the rate of 20 per cent is withheld at source from interest payment. This rate may be reduced or exempted by tax treaties.
V/11.111.1 V/11.112.1	Commercial banks acquiring funds and foreign currency deposits from non-resident banks	Income tax at the rate of 20 per cent is withheld at source from interest payment. This rate may be reduced or exempted by tax treaties. However, if an authorised foreign exchange bank receives loans or deposits in foreign currency from foreign central banks and the Japanese Government guarantees the repayment of them, the interest from the loans or deposits is exempted from income tax.

V.   PRINCIPAL SOURCES OF LEGAL AND REGULATORY PROVISIONS

Exchange Controls

- Foreign Exchange and Foreign Trade Control Law
  (Law No. 228, 1st Dec., 1949)

- Foreign Exchange Control Order
  (Cabinet Order 260 of 1980)

- Ministerial Ordinance concerning Control of Foreign Exchange
  (MOF Ordinance 44 of 1980)

- Ministerial Ordinance concerning Special Methods of Settlement
  (MOF Ordinance 48 of 1980)

- Cabinet Order concerning Direct Domestic Investments, etc.
  (Cabinet Order No. 251 of 11th October, 1980).

Minimum Reserve Requirement

- Law concerning Reserve Deposit Requirement System of 27th May, 1957.

Interest Rate Control

- Temporary Interest Rates Adjustment Law of 13th December, 1947.

Tax Regulations

- Income Tax Law

- Special Taxation Measures Law.

SPAIN

I. INTRODUCTION

(i)   Main characteristics of the regulatory system

As a matter of principle, all current and capital transactions
between residents and non-residents are subject to exchange control,
though in many cases they are carried out under general licences or
have been partly or completely liberalised. But even in such cases,
payments between residents and non-residents are subject to strict
control and have to be carried out through the intermediation of
"authorised banks". Out-payments are directly made by "authorised
banks" in the name of their resident customers, and the proceeds of
in-payments, when received directly by a resident, have to be sold to
an "authorised bank" within 15 days. All commercial and savings
banks may act to this effect as "authorised banks". (The Bank of
Spain plays a similar role but mainly restricted to non-convertible
currencies and to public sector foreign transactions).

"Authorised banks", when serving as a forced channel for payments between residents and non-residents, are acting, as a matter of
fact, as agencies of the Bank of Spain. They are free to apply the
foreign-exchange proceeds of authorised in-payments to authorised
out-payments, switching from one currency into another if necessary,
and they are able to sell foreign exchange to or get it from the
Bank of Spain. On balance, however, they are only allowed to hold
specifically limited foreign-exchange working balances, which the
Bank of Spain may ask them to surrender at any time.

However, "authorised banks" are at the same time subject, as
any other residents, to exchange control regulations in so far as
operations on their own account are concerned. Some regulations are
the same for banks and non-banks (e.g. those related to foreign
investment abroad or to borrowing abroad to switch the proceeds into
pesetas), while others are specific to "authorised banks" (e.g. borrowing and relending in foreign-currency or borrowing abroad in

50

pesetas). Such specific regulations are very liberal in the case of non-resident peseta accounts and rather permissive in the case of foreign-currency borrowing intended to finance foreign-currency loans to both non-residents (turntable operations (*)) and residents. But there are specific rules as to the net foreign-currency position resulting from operations carried out by banks on their account, which are in addition to those mentioned in the preceding paragraph.

This dual role of "authorised banks" and its different regulation, makes for some difficulties in the summary of regulations which is attempted below and should, therefore, be kept in mind when going through it. Though all commercial and savings banks may act as foreign-payments agents on account of the Bank of Spain, the ability to carry out foreign operations on their own account is restricted, in the case of a few commercial banks and all savings banks, not only by general exchange control regulations but by specific, mainly quantitative, limitations as well. These additional limitations are ignored throughout the following description, which refers only to those operations which may be carried out by banks enjoying full status as "authorised banks". Branches and affiliates of foreign banks have such a full status as "authorised banks" and are subject to the same regulations as domestic banks, though they are exempt from some prudential rules. Foreign branches (but not affiliates) of Spanish banks are subject to such regulations as well, though exception is made of local-currency operations with local residents.

The overall approach of exchange control to capital movements has traditionally been a rather liberal one in the case of long-term capital inflows and a very restrictive one in the case of long-term capital outflows. Such an attitude has to be traced back to a long history of current balance of payments deficits, coupled, up to a recent past, with a persistent low level of foreign central reserves. As a result of a dramatic improvement in the level of such reserves, some modest steps were taken at the end of 1979 to liberalize long-term capital outflows. The swing of the Spanish current account into a big deficit moved the authorities to liberalize even more the long-term capital inflows in 1980.

Regulations on bank short-term capital movements are also strongly biased in favour of net capital inflows. Capital inflows are allowed to a substantial extent, while capital outflows other than

_____

(*) In so far as these operations are concerned, regulations treat
     "authorised banks" in a certain way as off-shore banks. Such
     operations are excluded, for instance, from the official balance
     of payments.

those resulting from the unwinding of previous inflows are, as a rule, rather restricted. The authorities have, from time to time, modified either the regulations on short-term inflows or, when possible, their discretionary enforcement, in order to adjust net bank capital inflows to short-run balance of payments or monetary developments. In general, decisions prompted by exchange rate/balance of payments considerations have been more frequent than those based on pure domestic monetary developments, though the latter have tended to prevail during the recent period of balance of payments surpluses. Altogether, policy changes have not been very frequent and a substantial degree of variability in net bank short-term capital inflows has remained in response to relative monetary conditions in Spain and abroad. The importance of short-term capital movements in the balance of payments looks even larger when account is also taken of non-bank short-term capital movements linked to trade and to other current transactions, which, though legally restricted, may reach a substantial volume in either direction due to leads and lags resulting from legally permitted payment time lags (usually 3 or 6 months) and from a very sizeable volume of gross current transactions.

"Authorised banks" are not allowed to hold foreign-currency short positions, and foreign-currency long positions are permitted only within strict limits. A forward cover is, as a rule, required to avoid open positions in individual foreign currencies. There is no overall ceiling on the non-resident peseta position. The overall bank non-resident position is not regulated as such, but there is a fair amount of control on it through the regulation of its various components.

The administration of exchange control is, for historical reasons, split between the Ministry of Economy and Commerce and the Bank of Spain. As an approximate rule, the former is responsible for current transactions, trade credits and portfolio and direct investment flows, while the Bank of Spain is responsible for non-trade short-and long-term credits. Authority on the external transactions contemplated in the present document falls therefore, with minor exceptions, upon the Bank of Spain. However, regulations implemented by the Bank of Spain do not always stem from specific exchange-control legislation, since in some cases they arise out of its general bank regulatory and supervisory faculties.

International banking operations have, in general, a differential treatment as compared with domestic operations in such matters as reserve requirements, interest rate control and taxation.

Peseta deposits of non-bank residents with Spanish commercial and savings banks are subject to a minimum non-remunerated reserve requirement, which is the same for all kinds of institutions and for any type of deposits (present level 5.75 %). Special deposits with the Bank of Spain, remunerated at the discount rate (present level 8 %), have also been required on a temporary basis (present level 3 % of the above-mentioned liabilities). Both instruments are geared to the control of the money supply, and consequently do not apply to foreign-currency liabilities, non-resident peseta liabilities and inter-bank liabilities.

Interest rates on domestic-currency deposits of non-bank residents with a maturity up to 1 year are subject to legal ceilings, those with a maturity in excess on 1 year being free. Interest rates of foreign-currency deposits, interbank deposits and peseta deposits of non-residents are free. Similar regulations apply to banks' assets.

Interest payments on deposits of non-bank residents (irrespective of currency denomination) are subject to a 15 % withholding tax, while interbank deposits and non-resident deposits, whether in foreign- or in domestic-currency, are exempt therefrom. Banks are liable to a 3 % turnover tax on interest and fees received on any kind of claim on, and service provided to, residents, claims on non-residents being exempt.

(ii)   Selected data on international banking operations

Although Spain plays only a minor role in international financial markets, international operations of Spanish banks have in the 70's experienced a much faster growth than their domestic business. Total non-resident domestic- and foreign-currency liabilities of Spanish banks, which, as a percentage of their total liabilities (excluding capital accounts), amounted to 4,5 % in 1970, had grown to 7,4 % in 1973 and to 10,7 % in 1978. In absolute figures, total bank liabilities to non-residents amounted by the end of 1978 to about U.S. $ 14.5 billion, out of which 12.0 billion were in foreign-currencies and only 2.5 billion in domestic currency. Foreign assets of Spanish banks have shown a somewhat less rapid growth, and as of the end of 1978 they amounted to some U.S. $ 7.1 billions, most of them denominated in foreign currencies (*)

_____

(*)   The participation of savings banks in the above-quoted figures is very small. Foreign liabilities of commercial and industrial banks amounted, at the end of 1978, to 95 per cent of the total foreign liabilities of the banking system.

The net position of Spanish banks vis-à-vis non-residents has always been a net debtor position, and the Spanish banking system has been instrumental in channelling substantial capital inflows into the country. So, the net foreign liabilities of Spanish banks as of the end of 1978, amounting to about US $ 7.4 billion, may be compared with a net liability of about US $ 1.1 billion in 1973. Such capital inflows have been devoted mainly to fund foreign-currency bank loans to residents, of which some US $ 5.4 billion were outstanding at the end of 1978.

A comparison of the previous Spanish figures with the gross figures on external positions of banks in countries reporting to B.I.S. (which do not include Spain) shows that the role of Spanish banks in international markets is small. As of the end of 1978, foreign-currency liabilities of Spanish banks amounted to 2.3 per cent of those of twelve European reporting countries and total foreign liabilities of Spanish banks were equivalent to 1.6 per cent of total foreign liabilities of fourteen reporting countries and off-shore branches of US banks. Foreign assets of Spanish banks amounted on the same date to 0.8 per cent of total foreign assets as reported by B.I.S.

The peseta does not play any significant role as euro-currency, though some very limited euro-peseta operations are known to exist.

II. ANALYSIS OF REGULATIONS BY MAIN TYPES
OF CAPITAL MOVEMENTS

(situation at the end of January 1981)

(i)   Commercial banks' foreign-currency operations

(a) External foreign-currency borrowing for relending abroad

"Authorised banks" are, as a rule, free to accept foreign-
currency deposits from non-residents (both bank and non-bank) and
from other "authorised banks" provided that the proceeds are re-
deposited with non-resident banks or other "authorised banks",
relent to non-residents or applied to the purchase of foreign-currency
denominated money market paper or bonds (including the purchase in
foreign secondary markets of foreign-currency bonds issued by
Spanish residents). Foreign-currency borrowing through any instrument
other than deposits is subject to authorisation. Such turntable
operations are completely free of interest rate regulations, reserve
requirements or Spanish withholding taxes. However, the following
prudential regulations apply:

1. Outstanding foreign currency liabilities (excluding
deposits of other "authorised banks" but including such borrowing
as described under (e) below) may not exceed three times the volume
of banks' disbursed capital plus reserves.

2. Switching from one foreign currency into another is only
allowed on a swap basis or with a comparable forward cover of
principal plus interest.

3. The volume of foreign-currency claims on non-residents and
"authorised banks" maturing within any period has to be as a minimum
equal to 75 % of foreign-currency liabilities to non-residents and
"authorised banks" maturing within the same period.

4. Total claims on a single non-resident borrower may not
exceed 5 % of a bank's total foreign-currency liabilities nor 20 %
of a borrower's capital resources.

Foreign banks' branches and affiliates are exempt of these
prudential regulations. Other exceptions to any of these regulations
may be granted on an individual basis by the Bank of Spain.

(b) Capital inflows via inward switching

Foreign-currency borrowing and switching the proceeds of it
into pesetas is subject, in common with similar operations by non-
bank residents, to individual authorisation by the Bank of Spain.
Though the Bank of Spain has been rather liberal in granting such a
licence to non-bank residents (see (c) and (j) below), resident
banks have never asked for it, mainly because, as a result of forward
market regulations, no forward cover of such operations is possible.
The Bank of Spain has never purchased foreign currencies from banks
on a swap basis as an instrument to increase bank liquidity. To the
extent that "authorised banks" are allowed to hold small foreign-
exchange working balances there is, however, some limited scope to
switch into pesetas by selling them to the Bank of Spain.

(c) Capital inflows via the use of foreign-currency funds raised abroad for granting foreign-currency loans to resident non-banks

Foreign-currency borrowing as described under (a) and (e)
below may be used to finance foreign-currency loans to resident non-
banks, who actually do not receive any foreign exchange, as this is
simultaneously sold in the foreign-exchange market against pesetas.
Banks are not required to obtain any license to carry out such
operations, but they must make sure that the borrower does comply
with applicable exchange control regulations which are the same as
for borrowing from non-residents (*) and may imply an individual
license. So, trade import and export financing is carried out
under general licenses, but service export financing and non-trade
loans are subject to individual licenses, to the borrower. Interest
rates are free, and no reserve requirements are involved, but through
the licencing of these operations minimum or maximum maturities are
imposed. Licenses have, in general, been liberally granted. Only
in 1978 and especially in 1979, as a result of substantial balance-
of-payments surpluses, a more restrictive approach was developed
towards non-trade loans, whereby minimum maturities (initially 2
years and later on 4 years) and delays in carrying out the operation
were required (**). On the contrary, in 1980 the big current account

---

(*) Once again, "authorised banks" are, insofar as these operations
are concerned, treated to some extent as off-shore banks. The
borrower is free to choose between a resident or a non-resident
bank as the lender and, in the case of non-trade loans, the
currency denomination. (Once taken, these decisions are
embodied, however, into the licence terms).

(**) A 25 % non-remunerated reserve requirement was introduced in
April 1979, but was eliminated as of end-October 1979.

deficit moved the authorities to liberalize long-term capital inflows. According to this new policy, authorisation of long-term financial credits (of more than one year) is almost automatically granted. Taxation rules are the same as for peseta-denominated loans: no withholding tax on interest and 3 % turnover tax on interest and fees. (However, the same operations when financed by non-resident banks would be subject to a 24 % withholding tax and exempt from the turnover tax). No specific ceilings apply to the net foreign position deriving from these loans, and its indirect control through licenses to the borrowers is only approximate as a result of both the general character of some licenses and the freedom left in choosing, as the lender, between a resident bank or a non-resident. General credit ceilings on bank loans to residents (irrespective of currency denomination) were discontinued several years ago. As a result of these features, bank foreign-currency lending to residents tends to be very sensitive to relative monetary tightness in Spain and abroad and to exchange-rate expectations.

(d) Capital outflows via outward switching

Capital outflows through the purchase by banks of foreign exchange against pesetas is only possible on a very limited scale. To the extent that banks are authorised to keep small foreign exchange working balances, there may occasionally be some room to increase them. (There is no obligation of forward cover on these balances). Otherwise, short-term capital outflows would require individual licenses, which are not normally granted. However, mention should be made of the fact that in the recent past the Bank of Spain has occasionally had recourse to sales of foreign exchange against pesetas on a swap basis as a means of draining bank liquidity. But the scope of these operations, both in volume and in the number of banks involved, has been rather limited.

Medium- and long-term foreign-currency export credits to non-residents are allowed with an individual licence by the Ministry of Commerce, which is normally granted. Interest rate and maturity of such loans are determined by general export-credit regulations or by conditions set in the licence. The purchase of securities in foreign secondary markets has, as of recent, been liberalized up to the equivalent of 10 % of increases in each bank's disbursed capital plus reserves. Direct investments abroad, subject to individual licences, have normally been authorised in connection with the establishment of branches or affiliates abroad.

(e) <u>Capital outflows via financing external foreign-currency assets with foreign-currency deposits from resident non-banks</u>

Non-bank residents are now allowed, as a rule, to hold foreign-exchange deposits with resident banks, but in some cases (e.g. insurance companies, travel agencies, etc.) exceptions may be authorised.

To the extent that such deposits are permitted, they are counted as foreign borrowing to the effect of regulations described under (a) above, and it is therefore possible to relend their proceeds abroad. However, the net result of transactions under (a), (c) and (e), which are covered by the same set of regulations, has been a systematic and important net foreign-capital inflow.

(ii) <u>Commercial banks' domestic-currency operations with non-residents</u>

(f) <u>Domestic-currency liabilities to non-residents</u>

Originally, the regulation of non-resident deposits in pesetas was a rather liberal one, but as a result of restrictions on inward switching (see (b) above) Spanish banks made a growing use of such accounts as an alternative means of increasing their domestic liquidity. This led, from 1973 to the beginning of 1981 (with a very short liberalization spell between September 1977 and March 1978), to the imposition of very restrictive regulations. In January 1981, the regulation of non-resident peseta deposits has been liberalized. After this change non-resident peseta deposits belong in four different categories, with a specific regulation each, but only two of them have some relevance and deserve mention.

1. Convertible peseta accounts: they are freely convertible accounts which may be credited or debited by selling or buying foreign currency, by settlements derived from balance-of-payments transactions and by transfers between convertible peseta accounts. Overdrafts are forbidden unless due to mail. Any balance held on a convertible peseta account may be sold forward to the corresponding "authorised banks" on condition that it is maintained without interruption until the end of the forward contract. Authorised payments to non-residents in convertible pesetas are also entitled to forward cover by "authorised banks." Forward purchases of convertible pesetas by non-residents to "authorised banks" are free. Rules on net spot and forward positions in foreign exchange imply that net forward transactions in convertible pesetas against foreign exchange must be approximately in balance.

Balances on convertible peseta accounts are not subject to reserve requirements and their interest is free. No restrictions apply as to the maturity and the individual or overall size of such accounts. Regulations are the same, on the other hand, whether the non-resident depositor is a bank or a non-bank.

2. Emigrants accounts: non-resident Spaniards are entitled to open freely convertible peseta accounts (only in the form of passbook saving deposits), which may only be credited through sales of foreign exchange to "authorised banks". The interest paid on such deposits may not exceed a legal maximum, which, however, is substantially higher than the one applying to similar domestic deposits. Interest payments are exempt from the 15 % withholding tax and of any reserve requirement.

The purchase by non-residents of bank certificates of deposit (the only kind of money market paper issued by banks) is subject to authorization. On the contrary, the purchase by non-residents of long-term (5 to 10 years) bonds issued by some banks falls under the totally liberalized category of foreign portfolio investment (a 15 % withholding tax on interest payments applies to both residents and non-residents).

(g) Placing domestic-currency funds with foreign banks

These operations are explicitly forbidden.

(h) Domestic-currency credits and loans to non-resident non-banks

These transactions are subject to individual licence which, in general, is only granted (by the Ministry of Commerce) in the case of medium- and long-term export credits.

(iii) Non-bank borrowing and lending operations with non-resident banks

(j) Capital inflows via borrowing from non-resident banks

These transactions are covered by the same regulations as foreign-currency borrowing from resident banks, which are described under (c) above (they also apply to borrowing from non-resident non-banks).

(k) <u>Capital outflows via placing liquid assets with non-</u>
<u>resident banks</u>

Non-bank residents are not allowed, as a rule, to hold peseta and foreign-currency deposits with non-resident banks and a licence by the Ministry of Commerce would be required. However, there is an implicit possibility of marginal foreign-currency holdings to the extent that residents receiving foreign exchange on any account may delay up to 15 days its mandatory sale to "authorised banks".

III. SUMMARY VIEW OF REGULATIONS AND INSTRUMENTS AFFECTING INTERNATIONAL BANKING OPERATIONS OF BANKS AND NON-BANKS IN
SPAIN

(situation at end-January 1981)

Type of Operation or Balance Sheet Position / Type of Regulation or Instrument	Code	I. Exchange Control (1)	II. Minimum Reserve Requirements	III. Interest Rate Control	IV. Prudential Regulations	V. Tax Regulations	VI. Other Regulations or instruments
COMMERCIAL BANKS	1.						
Liability Operations/Positions	11.						
in foreign currencies	11.1						
with non-residents	11.11						
deposits from	11.111				x		
banks	11.111.1						
non-banks	11.111.2						
credits and loans from	11.112	x					
banks	11.112.1						
non-banks	11.112.2						
fixed-interest	11.113	x					
securities							
money market paper	11.113.1						
bonds	11.113.2						
with residents	11.12						
deposits from	11.121						
banks	11.121.1						
non-banks	11.121.2	x			x	x	
Central Bank or Government	11.121.3	x					
in domestic currency	11.2						
with non-residents	11.21						
current accounts of	11.211	x		x			
banks	11.211.1						
non-banks	11.211.2						
time deposits from	11.212	x		x			
banks	11.212.1						
non-banks	11.212.2						
credits and loans from	11.213	x					
banks	11.213.1						
non-banks	11.213.2						
fixed-interest securities	11.214						
money market paper	11.214.1	x					
bonds	11.214.2	x					x
Asset Operations/Positions	12.						
in foreign currencies	12.1						
with non-residents	12.11				x		
banks	12.111						
current accounts	12.111.1						
time deposits	12.111.2						
credits and loans	12.111.3			x			
non-banks	12.112						
credits and loans	12.112.1	x		x			
securities	12.113	x					
with residents	12.12						x
deposits with banks	12.121				x		
credits and loans to non-banks	12.122	x					
securities	12.123	x					
deposits with Central bank	12.124	x					

(1) And similar regulations imposing quantitative controls on capital transactions with non-residents.

(situation at end-January 1981)

Type of Operation or Balance Sheet Position / Type of Regulation or Instrument	Code	I. Exchange Control (1)	II. Minimum Reserve Requirements	III. Interest Rate Control	IV. Prudential Regulations	V. Tax Regulations	VI. Other Regulations or instruments
in domestic currency	12.2						
with non-residents	12.21						
deposits with banks	12.211	x					
credits and loans to	12.212	x		x			
banks	12.212.1						
non-banks	12.212.2						
securities	12.213	x					
Net Positions	13.						
in foreign currencies	13.1	x					
vis-à-vis non-residents	13.2						
NON-BANKS	2.						
Liability Operations/Positions	21.						
credits and loans from	21.1	x					
non-resident banks	21.11					x	
in foreign currencies	21.111						
in domestic currency	21.112						
resident banks	21.12						
in foreign currencies	21.121					x	
Asset Operations/Positions	22.						
with non-resident banks	22.1						
in foreign currencies	22.11	x					
current accounts	22.111						
time deposits	22.112						
in domestic currency	22.12						
deposits	22.121	x					
with resident banks	22.2						
in foreign currencies	22.21	x					
current accounts	22.211						
time deposits	22.212						
FOREIGN EXCHANGE OPERATIONS/POSITIONS	3.						
Commercial Banks	31.						
spot foreign exchange dealings	31.1	x					
forward foreign exchange dealings	31.2	x					
swap transactions	31.3	x					
net foreign exchange positions	31.4	x					
Non-Banks	32.						
spot foreign exchange dealings	32.1	x					
forward foreign exchange dealings	32.2	x					
swap transactions	32.3	x					

(1) And similar regulations imposing quantitative controls on capital transactions with non-residents.

(situation at the end of January 1981)

Code No. of classifica-tion schema	Operation/Position	Regulation

I. EXCHANGE CONTROL

Operations are free unless otherwise indicated, though those of "authorised banks" may be indirectly controlled through regulations on net foreign-currency positions.

Commercial banks

I/11.112 I/11.213	Foreign or domestic-currency borrowing from non-residents.	An individual authorisation by the Bank of Spain is required.
I/11.113	Foreign-currency money market paper or bond issues.	An individual licence by the Bank of Spain is required.
I/11.214.2	Sales of domestic-currency bonds to non-residents.	Issues in foreign markets (none has taken place up to now) would require an individual licence by the Bank of Spain, but non-resident purchases in the Spanish market are treated as entirely liberalized portfolio investments (more restrictive provisions apply to shares and convertible bonds).
I/12/112.1	Foreign-currency credits and loans to non-residents.	Free if financed with foreign-currency borrowing. Otherwise as in I/12.212.
I/12.113 I/12.123	Purchase of foreign-currency securities.	Fixed rate securities may be purchased without restrictions if financed by foreign-currency borrowing. Portfolio foreign investment through outward switching may freely take place up to 10 % of increases in bank's disbursed capital plus reserves. Otherwise, purchases are subject to individual licence (Prudential rules on total domestic and foreign-currency share holdings exist).

Code No. of classification Schema	Operations/Position	Regulation
I/11.121.2	Foreign-currency deposits of non-bank residents.	Only some residents (e.g. travel agencies, insurance companies) may hold such deposits subject to a licence by the Ministry of Commerce.
I/11.121.3 I/12.124	Foreign-currency deposits with or from the Central Bank	Only exceptionally have these operations been carried out, subject to ad-hoc rules. See, however, notes to I/31.4, as some foreign-currency working balances of "authorised banks" imply, in a sense, a foreign-currency liability to the Central Bank.
I/11.211 I/11.212	Non-resident domestic-currency demand and time deposits.	There are two main categories of "peseta accounts" with different regulations (see full description in section II (f)). Overdrafts are forbidden unless due to mail.
I/11.214.1	Sales of domestic-currency money market paper to non-residents.	The only relevant money market paper are certificates of deposit, and their sale to non-residents is implicitly forbidden through regulations on item 11.212.
I/12.122	Foreign-currency credits and loans to non-bank residents.	Banks are free to carry out such operations if financed by foreign-currency borrowing, but the borrower is subject to the same rules as in items 11.112, 11.213 and 21.11.
I/12.211	Domestic-currency deposits with non-resident banks.	They are forbidden.
I/12.212	Domestic-currency credits and loans to non-residents.	Subject to individual or general (some export-credit categories) licence. Only medium- and long-term export credits are normally authorised(by the Ministry of Commerce).
I/12.213	Purchase of securities in domestic currency from non-residents	Purchase of securities issued in the Spanish market would be free; issues in domestic currency by non-residents (subject to prior authorisation) have never taken place.
I/13.1	Net foreign-currency positions.	See I/31.4

Code No. of classification Schema	Operations/Position	Regulation
	Non-banks	
I/21.1	Foreign or domestic-currency borrowing from non-residents and foreign-currency borrowing from resident banks.	Trade-linked credits are subject to general or individual licences. by the Ministry of Commerce. Other credits require an individual authorisation by the Bank of Spain.
I/22.11	Foreign-currency deposits with non-resident banks.	An individual authorisation by the Ministry of Commerce is required.
I/22.121	Domestic-currency deposits with non-resident banks.	They are forbidden.
I/22.21	Foreign-currency deposits with resident banks.	See I/11.121.2
I.31.1	"Authorised banks" spot foreign-exchange dealings.	The following rules apply to foreign-exchange purchases and sales: A) With non-residents against other foreign currency: Free. B) With non-residents against pesetas: Free (see Section II, (f)). C) With other "authorised banks": Free against either foreign currency or domestic peseta accounts. D) With non-bank residents against foreign-currency: Forbidden. E) With non-bank residents against domestic peseta accounts: Purchases and sales are limited to authorised foreign transactions (see I/32.1).

Code No. of classification Schema	Operations/Position	Regulation
I.31.2	"Authorised banks" forward foreign-exchange dealings	Forward foreign-exchange transactions can only take place as cover for authorised external transactions, and the foreign-currency denomination has to be the same in both cases. Forward exchange maturities may not exceed in any case 12 months. The following additional rules apply to forward foreign-exchange purchases and sales: A) With non-residents against other foreign currency: Free, but only as needed to comply with regulations on spot or forward net positions (see I/31.4). B) With non-residents against convertible pesetas: Free under conditions stated in Section II, (g). C) With other "authorised banks" against domestic or foreign currency: As in A. D) With non-bank residents against other foreign currency: Forbidden. E) With non-bank residents against domestic peseta accounts: Purchases are free on account of any authorised in-payment but sales are restricted to trade import transactions.
I.31.3	"Authorised banks" swap transactions.	They are not explicitly regulated. There is no room for them with non-bank residents. In the case of non-residents they would be possible to the extent that both the spot and forward transaction fall under the rules described in I.31.1 and I.31.2. This means in practice freedom for foreign exchange/foreign exchange swaps, and, conditional to convertible peseta regulation for foreign exchange/ convertible peseta swaps.

Code No. of classification Schema	Operations/Position	Regulation
I.31.4	"Authorised banks" net foreign-exchange position	Foreign-currency direct and portfolio investment abroad, export credits or any other assets resulting from individually authorised outward switching are exempt from forward-cover requirements, net-position rules or global ceilings. Foreign-currency holdings linked to the "authorised banks" activity as payment agencies of the Bank of Spain (see Section I) are permitted up to a limit set for each bank by the Bank of Spain. No forward cover is required and the Bank of Spain, may ask banks to surrender such balances at any time. Except for mail overdrafts, short foreign-currency positions on any currency are forbidden. Otherwise (i.e. in relation to transactions described in Section II, (a), (c) and (e)), foreign-currency spot positions have to be covered, for each individual currency, by foreign-currency forward positions. The remaining foreign-currency forward operations (against domestic or for-eign-currency) are, subject to the following rules: open posi-tions in U.S. dollars exceeding U.S. $ 1,000,000 and exceeding the equivalent of $ 100,000 in each other individual currency are forbidden. Under special licence and up to a limit fixed by the Bank of Spain foreign-currency spot positions may temporarily be used as cover for forward domestic-currency purchases.
I/32.1	Non-bank spot foreign-exchange dealings.	Dealings are restricted to those with Spanish "authorised banks". Any foreign-currency receipts have to be surrendered to "authorised banks" within 15 days and purchases can only take place on account of authorised transactions.

Code No. of classification Schema	Operation/Position	Regulation
I/32.2	Non-bank forward exchange dealings.	Dealings are restricted to those with Spanish "authorised banks" Sales are free on account of any authorised in-payment but purchases can only take place on account of trade import transactions.
I/32.3	Non-bank swap transactions.	They are forbidden in any case.

II. MINIMUM RESERVE REQUIREMENTS

Foreign-currency deposits and domestic-currency non-resident deposits are exempt of reserve requirements, which, on the contrary, apply to domestic monetary liabilities (see Section I).

III. INTEREST RATE CONTROL

Unless otherwise specified, interest rates on foreign-currency operations and on non-resident domestic-currency operations are free.

III/11.211 III/11/212	Non-resident domestic-currency demand and time deposits with "authorised banks".	Payment of interest on so-called "Emigrants accounts" is subject to a ceiling (see Section II, f)
III/12.111.3 III/12.112.1	Foreign-currency bank) loans to non residents)	
III:12.212	) Domestic-currency bank) loans to non-residents.)	Interest rates on medium- and long-term export credits are subject to ceilings.

Code No. of classification Schema	Operation/Position	Regulation

IV.   PRUDENTIAL REGULATIONS

IV/11.111 IV/11.121.2	Foreign-currency deposits of non-residents and non-bank residents.	May not exceed three times the volume of banks' disbursed capital plus reserves.
IV/12.11 IV/12.121	Foreign-currency claims on non-residents and on resident "authorised banks".	When financed with foreign-currency borrowing, claims maturing within any period must be, at least, equal to 75 % of foreign-currency liabilities to non-residents and "authorised banks" maturing within the same period. Switching from one currency into another requires forward cover, and risk ceilings to individual claims also apply (see Section II, (a)).

V.   TAX REGULATIONS

Unless otherwise specified, interest payments on liabilities included in the table are exempt from the 15 % withholding tax, which, as a rule, applies in the case of payments to non-bank residents, and interest payments on assets are exempt from the 3 % turnover tax which applies to claims on residents.

V/11.121.2	Foreign-currency deposits of non-bank residents	)Interest payment is subject to)a 15 % withholding tax.
V/11.214.2	Sales by "authorised banks" of domestic-currency bonds.	)))
V/12.12	Foreign-currency claims on residents	Interest received by banks is subject to a 3 % turnover tax.
V/21.11	Credits and loans from non-resident banks to resident non-banks.	Interest payment is subject to a 24 % withholding tax.
V/21.121	Foreign-currency liabilities to resident banks.	See 12.12

V. PRINCIPAL SOURCES OF LEGAL AND REGULATORY PROVISIONS

Exchange Controls (and similar regulations imposing quantitative limitations on capital operations with non-residents)

1. Royal decree 2462/1980 of 10th October, 1980 on Foreign Exchange Controls.

2. Circular n. 9 of Foreign Department of the Bank of Spain, revised text of 1st April, 1980.

3. Circular n. 256 of Spanish Institute of Foreign Currency of 20th March, 1969.

4. Order of 23rd January, 1981.

5. Rules and regulations on Foreign Investments. Decree of 31st October, 1974.

6. Decree on Spanish Investments abroad of 14th September, 1979.

7. Circular n. 10 of Foreign Department of the Bank of Spain, revised text of 30th January, 1981.

III. Interest Rate Control
Order of 17th January, 1981.

IV. Prudential Regulations
Circular n. 9 of the Foreign Department of the Bank of Spain, revised text of 1st April, 1980.

V. Tax Regulations
Act of 27th December, 1978
Act of 8th September, 1978

Act of 25th September, 1979
Decree of 21st December 1979

UNITED STATES

I. INTRODUCTION

(i)   Main purposes of the regulatory system

U.S. banking regulations, which, in general, treat liabilities
to U.S. and non-U.S. depositors identically, are designed mainly to
assist monetary policy in the achievement of domestic goals, to prevent substantial competitive inequities, and to promote the safety
and soundness of banks. Hence, they are not specifically directed
toward exchange-rate or balance-of-payments objectives.

From 1965 to early 1974, the United States had a system of
capital controls covering banks and certain financial and nonfinancial
institutions. The objective of the controls was to moderate deficits
in the U.S. balance of payments. Those controls were eliminated in
January 1974. Thus the United States no longer regulates capital
outflows to achieve international objectives.

The U.S. Banking System. Banking institutions in the United
States operate under a complex regulatory system. Fifty State
banking agencies and one Federal agency, the Office of the Comptroller
of the Currency (OCC), grant charters for banks and issue licences
for U.S. branches and agencies of foreign banks. In addition, the
Federal Reserve Board grants charters for Edge Act corporations,
which are restricted to an international banking business and are
subject to the same reserve requirements as banks that are members
of the Federal Reserve System(1). The fifty States supervise jointly
with the Federal Reserve the 1,000 state-chartered banks that are
voluntary members of the Federal Reserve System and supervise jointly
with the Federal Deposit Insurance Corporation (FDIC) the 8.700

---

(1) State-chartered Agreement corporations, which have an insignificant
    volume of business, agree to be subject to Federal Reserve regula-
    tion, which restricts their banking powers to those of Edge
    Corporations.

state-chartered banks that are voluntary members of the Federal Reserve System and supervise jointly with the Federal Deposit Insurance Corporation (FDIC) the 8,700 state-chartered nonmember banks that maintain FDIC insurance(1). The OCC supervises the 4,600 national banks, which are required to be members of the Federal Reserve System and to carry FDIC insurance. Branches and agencies of foreign banks are supervised by their licensing authority and are subject, under the International Banking Act of 1978, and under the Monetary Control Act of 1980, to reserve requirements and interest-rate limitations on deposits and credit balances as determined by the Federal Reserve Board(2). The Federal Reserve Board also regulates bank holding companies and their nonbanking activities. It also has residual power to examine subsidiary banks normally examined by the OCC, the FDIC, or by State banking authorities. This country note will discuss only Federal regulations since with few exceptions the 9,000 state-chartered nonmember banks conduct virtually no international business.

Federal Banking Regulations. There are two basic types of Federal banking regulations that affect, but generally are not designed to regulate, international banking operations. First, there are regulations prescribing maximum interest rates that depository institutions can pay on certain deposit liabilities and other borrowings. Second, there are reserve requirements on deposit liabilities and on certain other bank liabilities (borrowings) of depository institutions that have been defined as deposits for purposes of applying reserve requirements(3).

By law, no interest is paid on demand deposits. Regulations prescribing maximum interest rates on various other types of deposits are complex. Most notable for this note are the restrictions on deposits with maturities of less than 14 days. Specifically, the highest interest payable on a deposit account with a maturity of less

---

(1) There are about 300 uninsured state-chartered nonmember banks. Also, the State of New York regulates several uninsured investment companies that are chartered under Article XII of the New York Banking Law and that are owned directly or indirectly by foreign banks. Their banking powers are roughly similar to those of agencies.

(2) A branch that is licensed by a State and carries FDIC insurance will be supervised jointly by the State and the FDIC.

(3) The Board is authorized to apply reserve requirements only to deposit liabilities of financial institutions. However, the authorization allows the Board to determine what liabilities shall be deemed deposits for such purposes. In this note, the terminology for reservable liabilities will include deposits (as such), reservable borrowings (other reservable liabilities), and deposits for reserve purposes (deposits and reservable borrowings combined).

than 14 days is 5-1/4 per cent on a NOW (Negotiable Order of With-drawal) accounts. The maximum rates prescribed by regulation for deposits with longer maturities are believed to affect primarily the form of liabilities that arise from international banking transactions rather than the volume of such liabilities at U.S. offices. The Board and FDIC have exempted from ceilings certain time deposits of foreign governments and certain international organizations and have suspended the maximum rates on time deposits held by all others when in denominations of $ 100,000 or more. Moreover, also exempted by regulation from rate ceilings are all borrowings from other banks, liabilities arising from repurchase transactions involving U.S. Government securities, and liabilities meeting the regulatory requirements of subordinated debt. Accordingly, the interest rates payable on most liabilities to other banks, corporations, foreign governments, wealthy individuals, and so forth are not subject to ceilings and are market-determined rates, either because the Board and FDIC have suspended the ceilings, as on time deposits at $ 100,000 or more, or because they have exempted from ceilings specific deposits or borrowings that are close substitutes for liabilities that have interest-rate ceilings.

Reserve requirements raise a bank's cost of funding earning assets because the assets held to satisfy these reserve requirements, namely vault cash and deposits at Federal Reserve Banks, do not bear interest. The Monetary Control Act of 1980 subjected all deposi-tory institutions, including member and nonmember commercial banks, savings banks, savings and loan associations and credit unions, to Federal reserve requirements. Reserve requirements under the Monetary Control Act are being phased-in with details of the phase-in depen-ding on the class of institution and the type of liability. In general, the reserve requirements for member banks are being phased-in from the requirements previously in effect over a period of approx-imately 3-1/2 years ending in March 1983. Reserve requirements for U.S. branches and agencies of foreign banks are being phased-in over a two-year period ending in August 1982; and reserve requirements for nonmember depository institutions are being phased-in over a period of 7 years and one day ending in September 1987. Under the Monetary Control Act, reserve requirements are applied to net trans-actions accounts, nonpersonal time deposits, and Eurocurrency liabilities, and other money market liabilities such as ineligible acceptances and funds obtained from bank holding companies.

Transactions accounts generally include demand deposits, NOW (Negotiable Order of Withdrawal) accounts, and Automatic Transfer Service (for transfers of funds from savings to demand accounts) and other accounts that can be used to effect payments to third parties. Accounts held by U.S. and foreign residents are treated identically. Net transactions accounts are gross transactions accounts minus the sum of cash items in the process of collection and gross demand balances due from other depository institutions in the United States. After the phase-in the reserve requirement will be 3 per cent on the first $ 25 million of an institutions's net transactions accounts and 12 per cent on any net transactions accounts over $ 25 million. The board is authorized to vary the reserve ratio on transactions accounts in excess of $ 25 million within a range of 8 to 14 per cent. In addition, in 1982 the $ 25 million amount will increase or decrease by 80 per cent of the percentage change in total transaction accounts in the banking system.

Nonpersonal time deposits are defined as transferable time deposits or accounts, or time deposits or accounts in which any beneficial interest is held by an agency who is not an individual or a sole proprietor. There is no distinction drawn between deposits held by U.S. and foreign residents. After the phase-in the reserve requirement will be 3 per cent on nonpersonal time deposits with original maturities of less than 4 years and 0 per cent on nonpersonal time deposits with original maturities of 4 years of more (1). The Board can vary the reserve requirement ratio on nonpersonal time deposits within a range of zero to nine per cent.

The Eurocurrency reserve requirements are designed to eliminate artificial incentives favoring the raising of funds offshore as compared with raising funds in the domestic markets. Gross borrowings by institutions in the United States from unaffiliated foreign depository institutions are subject to requirements that, after the phase-in period, will reach 3 per cent. This ratio applies also to

---

(1) In addition to interest ceilings and reserve requirements there is an assessment for deposit insurance. The Federal Deposit Insurance Corporation is authorized by law to levy a deposit insurance assessment on all national banks, all state-chartered member banks, and those state-chartered nonmember banks that have chosen to carry FDIC deposit insurance. In recent years the net assessment paid by insured banks equalled about 1/26 of one per cent of assessable deposits, which do not include, among other liabilities, deposits at foreign offices. The FDIC is also authorized, by the International Banking Act of 1978, to levy a deposit-insurance assessment on a U.S. branch of a foreign bank when the branch is deemed to be engaged in domestic retail deposit activities (in general, when it accepts deposits in denominations of less than $ 100,000 unless exempted by the OCC, if Federally licenced, or by the FDIC if State licenced).

the sum of proceeds of sales of domestic or foreign assets to an institutions' own foreign offices, loans to U.S. residents made by foreign offices of depository institutions organized under U.S. law, and balances due to a U.S. institution's non-U.S. offices less amounts due from the institution's non-U.S. offices.

Effective December 3, 1981 U.S. banking offices of both foreign and domestically-owned banking institutions will be allowed to establish International Banking Facilities (IBFs). These facilities may accept deposits from and extend credit to foreign residents or other IBFs. All such deposits will be exempt from reserve requirements and interest rate ceilings. Advances by an IBF to U.S. offices of its parent institution will be subject to the Eurocurrency reserve requirement mentioned above. IBF deposits must support customer operations outside the United States. Deposits that IBFs receive from nonbanks require a minimum of two days notice for withdrawal, and all IBF deposits and withdrawals must be for at least $ 100,000. Loans at IBFs are to be used to finance non-U.S. operations. IBF loans and deposits may be denominated in any currency. It is hoped that IBF's will enhance the international competitive position of banking institutions located in the United States but not interfere with the achievement of domestic monetary policy objectives.

Finally, banks chartered under National Law (National Banks) are subject to a limit on loans to any single borrower of 10 per cent of capital and surplus. This limit applies to loans to foreign or domestic borrowers. The Comptroller of the Currency has ruled that the aggregate of all loans to official borrowers in any country made by a National bank will be subject to this 10 per cent limitation unless a borrowing entity can show that it has an independent source of revenue and separate use for the funds(1). Banks chartered under state laws are subject to the laws of individual states governing their loans to official foreign borrowers.

Federal taxation. Under Federal tax law, the U.S. Government imposes, in general, a withholding tax of 30 per cent on payments of interest and dividends from U.S. sources to non-resident aliens and foreign corporations. The withholding tax assures that these income

---

(1) The three Federal banking agencies have instituted a common approach to supervising banks' exposure to country risk, as distinct from commercial risk. The primary emphasis is to encourage portfolio diversification and to point out to a bank's senior official and directors concentrations of lending measured in relation to capital. There are no mandatory lending limits under this country-exposure examination system.

recipients pay U.S. Federal tax if their interest and dividend income is subject to U.S. Federal taxes. There are several ways, however, in which such income can be shielded from the full 30 per cent withholding-tax rate.

Most notable in terms of U.S. international banking operations, interest income of non-resident aliens, including foreign governments, on bank deposits in the United States is statutorily exempt from the withholding tax.

The withholding tax rate is also reduced in some cases through tax treaties between the United States and foreign countries. Examples of actual withholding rates applying to interest payments from U.S. sources to entities specified in different treaties are 5 per cent for Switzerland and zero per cent for Germany, the United Kingdom, and the Netherlands (and the Netherlands Antilles).

In addition to the statutory exemption of deposit interest earned by non-resident aliens and the reduction in, or exemption from, withholding taxes under tax treaties, U.S. tax law also, under certain circumstances, exempts from withholding tax interest payments by resident alien individuals or U.S. corporations located in the United States if such persons or corporations have less than 20 per cent of their gross income for the preceding three years from sources within the United States. An example is international finance subsidiaries, some of which have been called "Delaware corporations" and have been set up by U.S. banks in the past.

(ii)   Selected data on international banking operatings

Banks operating in the United States, including branches and agencies of foreign banks, conduct a large and varied international banking business, nearly all of which is denominated in U.S. dollars. External claims payable in foreign currencies totalled $ 2.9 billion, and external liabilities were $ 6.1 billion at the end of December 1980(1).

External claims of banking offices located in the United States grew from $ 18.1 billion in December 1973, just before U.S. capital controls were removed, to $ 187.0 billion in December 1980. During those eight years their external liabilities, which had been

_____

(1) Figures derived from the Treasury Bulletin.

free of controls, grew from $ 32.6 billion to $ 159.7 billion(1).In comparison with domestic business of banking offices in the United States, international business expanded much more rapidly. External assets grew about 930 per cent, external liabilities about 390 per cent, and internal assets and liabilities about 80 and 90 per cent respectively during the eight years. As a result, external assets increased from 2.6 per cent of total assets at end 1973 to 12.8 per cent in December of 1980. External liabilities as a per cent of total liabilities rose from 4.6 per cent to 11.0 per cent(2). The increase in external assets reflects in part a catching up in domestic booking of international credits after capital controls were removed in January 1974 and, more fundamentally, the general internationalization of banking worldwide during the 1970s coupled with relatively less expensive credit conditions in the United States during the period as a whole.

Also notable during the period was the rapid growth in U.S. operations of foreign banks - at a rate considerably faster than that of U.S. banks' domestic offices. Total assets of all U.S. offices of foreign banks (including subsidiary commercial banks) rose from about $ 30 billion to more than $ 200 billion between December 1973 and December 1980. The size and growth of the foreign banks' U.S. activities, as well as their ability to open deposit-taking offices in more than one state, were major factors leading to passage of the International Banking Act of 1978. That Act created a Federal supervisory and regulatory structure for U.S. branches and agencies of foreign banks, which had previously been supervised and regulated almost entirely by the states.

---

(1) U.S. banks' operations in foreign countries have also grown rapidly during the period. Claims of foreign branches nearly tripled and stood at $ 292 billion in September of 1980. Seventy per cent were payable in U.S. dollars. The figure does not include claims on U.S. parent banks and on other foreign branches of each reporting banks.

(2) Figures derived from data published in IMF International Financial Statistics on Commercial Banks.

II. ANALYSIS OF REGULATIONS BY MAIN TYPES OF CAPITAL MOVEMENTS

(situation at the end of 1980)

(i)   Commercial Banks' Foreign-Currency Operations

    (a)   External foreign-currency borrowing for relending abroad

The United States imposes no restrictions specifically on foreign-currency borrowing by a U.S. banking office for relending abroad.

The Board of Governors of the Federal Reserve System, in 1973 and again in 1975 stated, in response to a bank's inquiry, that issuance of foreign-currency denominated time deposits by member banks at their offices in the United States would not be in the public interest because development of the practice "could at times pose an increased threat to the international stability of the dollar." Deposits in IBFs can, however, be denominated in either dollars or foreign currency.

Interest earned by non-residents on foreign-currency (and dollar) bank deposits in the United States is statutorily exempt from the U.S. withholding tax on interest payments to foreigners. (See Sections I and IV for details on tax withholding on interest earned on non-deposit liabilities.)

    (b)   Capital inflows via inward switching

Treatment of these inflows is the same as in (i)(a) above.

    (c)   Capital inflows via the use of foreign-currency funds raised abroad for granting foreign-currency loans to resident non-banks

Treatment of these inflows is the same as in (i)(a) above.

    (d)   Capital outflows via outward switching

The U.S. Government imposes no legal restrictions or administrative guidelines on outflows into foreign-currency assets.

    (e)   Capital outflows via financing external foreign-currency assets with foreign currency deposits from resident non-banks

Treatment of the outflow is the same as in (i)(d) above. Treatment of the foreign-currency deposit is the same as in (i)(a) above.

(ii)   Commercial Banks' Domestic-Currency Operations with
       Non-Residents
       (f)   Domestic-currency liabilities to non-residents
       Banks' liabilities to non-residents are subject to reserve
requirements, except for liabilities that are deposits in or borrowings by IBF's. Inflows in the form of a bank's borrowings from
foreign banks and of increases in a bank's net liabilities to its own
foreign branches or IBF's are subject to reserve requirements. The
reserve ratios have been varied, usually for purposes of domestic
monetary policy and equity but occasionally for international
purposes. Under the Monetary Control Act the reserve ratio on these
transactions is being phased-in to 3 per cent. Inflows in the form
of nonpersonal time deposits and transactions accounts are subject
to the general reserve requirements that are also applied to deposits
and accounts of U.S. residents, described in Section I.

       With the exception of IBFs, these inflows into banks are also
generally subject to the usual interest-rate ceilings, described in
Section I and shown in Section V. The Federal Reserve Board and
FDIC, however, have long exempted certain time deposits of selected
foreign official institutions from ceilings on the maximum interest
rates payable on time deposits. Specifically exempt are time deposits
having a maturity of two years or less and representing funds deposited
and owned by (1) a foreign national government and its agencies
engaged principally in activities that are ordinarily performed in the
United States by governmental entities, (2) an international entity
of which the United States is a member, or (3) any other foreign,
international, or supranational entity specifically designated by the
Board and FDIC as exempt. Also, the Board and FIDC have suspended the
maximum interest rates on all liabilities (including borrowings)
classified as time deposits when in denominations of $ 100,000 or
more, regardless of maturity. Also exempt from interest-rate
ceilings are borrowings from U.S. offices of banks (Federal funds
purchases), borrowings from foreign offices of other banks,
liabilities arising from repurchase agreements involving securities
of the U.S. Government and its agencies, and liabilities meeting the
regulatory requirements of subordinated debt. Accordingly, the
interest rates payable on most liabilities to corporations, foreign
governments, and wealthy individuals are market-determined rates
and not subject to ceilings.

       Interest earned by non-residents on dollar- (and foreign-)
currency denominated bank deposits in the United States is statutorily
exempt from the U.S. withholding tax on interest payments to foreigners

(See Section I and IV for details on tax withholding on interest earned on non-deposit liabilities.)

(g) Placing domestic-currency funds with foreign banks
The U.S. government applies no legal restrictions or administrative guidelines to outflows into U.S. dollar assets.

(h) Domestic currency credits and loans to non-resident non-banks
The U.S. Government applies no legal restrictions or administrative guidelines to outflows into U.S. dollar assets.

(iii) Non-Bank Borrowing and Lending Operations with Non-Resident Banks

(j) Capital inflows via borrowing from non-resident banks
In general, the U.S. Government imposes no regulatory restrictions or disincentives on capital inflows to a U.S. nonbank from non-resident banks. But when a foreign branch of a U.S. member lends to a U.S. non-bank, then the U.S. head office of the member bank is subject to a reserve requirement against deposits in its foreign branch equal to the amount of the loan to the U.S. non-bank resident. Ultimately the reserve ratio will be 3 per cent. To reduce the administrative burden on banks, there are two exemptions. A foreign branch's loans aggregating $ 100,000 or less to any U.S. resident are excluded from reserve computations, as are any branch's total loans to U.S. residents if they do not exceed $ 1 million in aggregate. These provisions reduce the administrative burden for branches that do not regularly make significant amount of loans to U.S. residents. In addition to these provisions, to the extent that foreign branch loans to U.S. non-bank borrowers are matched by net advances of funds from a bank's head office to its foreign branches, the loans are exempt from reserve requirements.

(k) Capital inflows via placing liquid assets with non-resident banks
A nonbank in the United States is free of U.S. Government legal restrictions and administrative guidelines when it places liquid assets with any banking institution in other countries. The Federal Reserve System, however, has stated that it would be inappropriate for a member bank to solicit or encourage the placement of deposits by United States residents at its foreign branches unless such deposits are placed to serve a definite, necessary purpose outside the United States.

(situation at the end of 1980)

Type of Operation or Balance Sheet Position	Code	I. Exchange Control (1)	II. Minimum Reserve Requirements	III. Interest Rate Control	IV. Prudential Regulations	V. Tax Regulations	VI. Other Regulations or instruments
COMMERCIAL BANKS	1.						
Liability Operations/Positions	11.		X	X			
in foreign currencies	11.1						X
with non-residents	11.11						
deposits from	11.111					X	
banks	11.111.1		X				
non-banks	11.111.2			X			
credits and loans from	11.112					X	
banks	11.112.1		X	X			
non-banks	11.112.2			X			
fixed-interest securities	11.113						
money market paper	11.113.1					X	
bonds	11.113.2		X	X		X	
with residents	11.12						
deposits from	11.121						
banks	11.121.1						
non-banks	11.121.2						
Central Bank or Government	11.121.3						
in domestic currency	11.2						
with non-residents	11.21						
current accounts of	11.211						
banks	11.211.1		X				
non-banks	11.211.2			X			
time deposits from	11.212					X	
banks	11.212.1		X				
non-banks	11.212.2			X			
credits and loans from	11.213					X	
banks	11.213.1		X	X			
non-banks	11.213.2			X			
fixed-interest securities	11.214						
money market paper	11.214.1					X	
bonds	11.214.2		X	X		X	
Asset Operations/Positions	12.						
in foreign currencies	12.1						
with non-residents	12.11						
banks	12.111						
current accounts	12.111.1						
time deposits	12.111.2						
credits and loans	12.111.3						
non-banks	12.112						
credits and loans	12.112.1						
securities	12.113						
with residents	12.12						
deposits with banks	12.121						
credits and loans to non-banks	12.122						
securities	12.123						
deposits with Central bank	12.124						

(1) And similar regulations imposing quantitative controls on capital transactions with non-residents.

III. SUMMARY VIEW OF REGULATIONS AND INSTRUMENTS AFFECTING INTERNATIONAL
BANKING OPERATIONS OF BANKS AND NON-BANKS IN

THE UNITED STATES

(Contd.)   (situation at the end of 1980)

Type of Operation or Balance Sheet Position / Type of Regulation or Instrument	Code	I. Exchange Control (1)	II. Minimum Reserve Requirements	III. Interest Rate Control	IV. Prudential Regulations	V. Tax Regulations	VI. Other Regulations or instruments
in domestic currency	12.2						
with non-residents	12.21						
deposits with banks	12.211						
credits and loans to	12.212						
banks	12.212.1						
non-banks	12.212.2						
securities	12.213						
Net Positions	13.						
in foreign currencies	13.1						
vis-à-vis non-residents	13.2						
NON-BANKS	2.						
Liability Operations/ Positions	21.						
credits and loans from	21.1						
non-resident banks	21.11		X			X	
in foreign currencies	21.111						
in domestic currency	21.112						
resident banks	21.12						
in foreign currencies	21.121						
Asset Operations/Positions	22.						
with non-resident banks	22.1						X
in foreign currencies	22.11						
current accounts	22.111						
time deposits	22.112						
in domestic currency	22.12						
deposits	22.121						
with resident banks	22.2						
in foreign currencies	22.21						
current accounts	22.211						
time deposits	22.212						X
FOREIGN EXCHANGE OPERATIONS/ POSITIONS	3.						
Commercial Banks	31.						
spot foreign exchange dealings	31.1						
forward foreign exchange dealings	31.2						
swap transactions	31.3						
net foreign exchange positions	31.4						
Non-Banks	32.						
spot foreign exchange dealings	32.1						
forward foreign exchange dealings	32.2						
swap transactions	32.3						

(1) And similar regulations imposing quantitative controls on capital transactions with
non-residents.

Code No. of classi- fication schema	Operation/ Position	Regulation

II. MINIMUM RESERVE REQUIREMENTS

II/11.	Commercial banks' liability oper- ations/ positions (in foreign and domestic currencies)	Without regard to currency denomi- nation or residence of depositors, the first $ 25 million of an institutions net transactions ac- counts will ultimately be subject to a 3 per cent reserve require- ment while the remaining trans- actions accounts will ultimately be subject to 12 per cent reserve requirement. (For details of the phase-in see Section I.
		Reserve requirements on nonper- sonal time deposits with maturities of less than 4 years will ulti- mately be subject to a 3 per cent reserve requirement. (For details of the phase-in see Section I.
		Deposits at IBFs are exempt from reserve requirements.
II/11.111.1 II/11.112.1* II/11.211.1* II/11.212.1 II/11.213.1	Commercial banks' foreign currency credits and loans from non-resident banks and dollar current accounts of non-resident banks	A member bank's domestic office net liabilities to its own foreign branches and IBFs and gross liabilities to unaffiliated foreign depository institutions will ultimately be subject to a 3 per cent reserve requirement.
II/21.11	Resident non-banks taking credits and loans from non- resident banks	As a companion to the reserve requirement under codes II/11.112.1 and II/11.211.1, a member bank's deposit liabilities at its foreign branches can be subject to a reserve requirement. The reserv- able amount equals the credits and loans outstanding to U.S. residents that the foreign branches have extended or have acquired from a U.S. office of the member bank. Excluded from the calculation of reservable branch liabilities are credits and loans extended in the aggregate amount of $ 100,000 or less to any U.S. resident and credits and loans of any branch that has total credit to U.S. residents of $ 1 million or less.

*/
This code is shown for more than one specific operation or position regulated by minimum reserve requirements.

Code No. of classi-fication schema	Operation/ Position	Regulation
II/11.113.2 II/11.214.2	Fixed-interest bonds (also variable-rate bonds)	An obligation (with fixed or variable interest rate) subordinated to claims of depositors and meeting specific conditions of minimum maturity and minimum face amount, among other conditions, are treated as capital and are not subject to reserve requirements.

III. INTEREST RATE CONTROL

III/11.	Commercial banks' liability operations/positions (in foreign and domestic currencies)	The maximum rate payable on a deposit with an original maturity of less than 14 days is 5-1/4 per cent. FDIC insured banks are subject to regulations that prescribe maximum interest rates payable on time deposits and certain non-deposit liabilities (borrowings). The maximum rate payable on savings deposits is 5-1/4 per cent and on other time deposits and borrowings varies according to the type of deposit and its original maturity. Maximum rates have been suspended, however, on time deposits and borrowings in denominations of $ 100,000 or more and on deposits at IBFs. In addition, liabilities arising from Federal funds purchases and repurchase transactions involving U.S. Government securities are, by regulation, exempt from interest rate ceilings.
II/11.112.1 II/11.213.1	Liabilities to banks	All nondeposit liabilities to banks are, by regulation, exempt from interest-rate ceilings.
III/11.111.2 III/11.112.2 III/11.211.2 III/11.212.2 III/11.213.2	Time deposits of foreign governmental entities and international organizations	Also exempt from interest-rate ceilings are time deposits with original maturity of two years or less when the deposits have been issued to and are owned by (1) a foreign national government and its agencies engaged principally in activities that are ordinarily performed in the United States by governmental entities, (2) an international entity of which the United States is a member, or (3) any other foreign, international, or supranational entity specifically designated by the Board as exempt.

Code No. of classi- fication schema	Operation/ Position	Regulation
		Since mid-1973, however, the maximum-rate ceilings have been suspended on all time deposits in denominations of $ 100,000 or more irrespective of their owner- ship or their maturity.
III/11.113.2 III/11.214.2	Fixed-interest bonds (also variable-rate bonds)	An obligation (with fixed or vari- able interest rate) subordinated to claims of depositors and meeting specific conditions of minimum maturity, repayment schedule, and minimum face amount, among other conditions, is treated as capital and is exempt from interest-rate ceilings.

V. TAX REGULATIONS

V/11.111 V/11.212	Deposits from non-residents	Interest income of non-resident aliens on bank deposits in the United States is statutorily exempt from U.S. withholding tax.
V/11.112 V/11.213	Credits and loans in foreign curren- cies or dollars to commercial banks from non-resident banks and non- resident nonbanks.	Interest payments are subject to a 30 per cent statutory withholding tax, except as reduced by tax treaty.
V/11.113.1 V/11.214.1	Money market paper issued in foreign currencies or dollars by commer- cial banks and held by non-residents	Original issue discount is exempt from withholding tax for corporate instruments with an original term of less than six months. All other interest payments are subject to a 30 per cent statutory withholding tax, except as reduced by tax treaty.
V/11.113.2 V/11.214.2	Bonds issued in foreign currencies or dollars by com- mercial banks and held by non-residents	Interest payments are subject to a 30 per cent statutory withholding tax, except as reduced by tax treaty or except when paid by an international finance subsidiary of a bank (see Section I).
V/21.11	Credits and loans in foreign curren- cies or dollars to non-banks from non- resident banks	Interest payments are subject to a 30 per cent statutory withholding tax, except as reduced by tax treaty or except when paid by an international finance subsidiary of a bank (see Section I).

Code No. of classi- fication schema	Operation/ Position	Regulation

VI. OTHER REGULATIONS OR INSTRUMENTS

VI/11.1 VI/22.212	Time deposits pay- able in a foreign currency or foreign currencies	There are no legal restrictions on a bank that holds assets or issues liabilities payable in a foreign currency or currencies. But the Board of Governors of the Federal Reserve System, in 1973 and again in 1975, stated in response to a bank's inquiry that issuance of foreign-currency denominated time deposits at a U.S. office would not be in the public interest. It stated that development of the practice "could at times pose an increased threat to the inter-national stability of the dollar."
VI/22.1	Deposits of U.S. residents at foreign branches of member banks	The Board of Governors of the Federal Reserve System, through letters signed by Chairman Martin and Chairman Burns and through a press release in 1978, has stated that it would be inappropriate for a member bank to solicit or encourage the placement of deposit by United States residents at its foreign branches unless such deposits are placed to serve a definite, necessary purpose out-side the United States. U.S. non-bank residents themselves are free to hold deposits in any banking office abroad.

V.   PRINCIPAL SOURCES OF LEGAL AND REGULATORY PROVISIONS

Reserve requirements
>   Section 19 of the Federal Reserve Act (12 USC 461) and
>   Regulation D of the Federal Reserve Board (12 CFR 204).

Interest-rate ceilings on liabilities
>   Section 19 of the Federal Reserve Act (12 USC 461),
>   Regulation Q of the Federal Reserve Board (12 CFR 217), and
>   Published Interpretations of the Federal Reserve Board,
>   paragraph 3390

Discouragement of member banks from issuing time deposits denominated
    in foreign currency
>   Federal Reserve Board letter to John J. Balles, president,
>   Federal Reserve Bank of San Francisco, dated January 8, 1975.

Admonition against soliciting and encouraging deposits of U.S. resi-
    dents at foreign branches.
>   Letters to member banks with foreign branches from Chairman
>   Wm. McC. Martin, Jr., dated June 3, 1969, and from Chairman
>   Arthur F. Burns, dated July 21, 1975.
>   Federal Reserve Board press release dated August 28, 1978.

Withholding tax
>   Section 1441 of Internal Revenue Code of 1954 and appropriate
>   tax treaties.

Interest income from bank deposits in the United States
>   Section 861 and 892 of Internal Revenue Code of 1954.

International financial subsidiaries
>   Section 861 (a1B) of Internal Revenue Code of 1954.

OECD SALES AGENTS
DÉPOSITAIRES DES PUBLICATIONS DE L'OCDE

GENTINA – ARGENTINE
los Hirsch S.R.L., Florida 165, 4° Piso (Galería Guemes)
33 BUENOS AIRES, Tel. 33.1787.2391 y 30.7122

USTRALIA – AUSTRALIE
stralia and New Zealand Book Company Pty, Ltd.,
Aquatic Drive, Frenchs Forest, N.S.W. 2086
. Box 459, BROOKVALE, N.S.W. 2100

USTRIA – AUTRICHE
CD Publications and Information Center
imrockstrasse 5300 BONN. Tel. (0228) 21.60.45
cal Agent/Agent local :
rold and Co., Graben 31, WIEN 1. Tel. 52.22.35

LGIUM – BELGIQUE
LS
avenue de Stalingrad, 1000 BRUXELLES. Tel. 02.512.89.74

AZIL – BRÉSIL
stre Jou S.A., Rua Guaipa 518,
ita Postal 24090, 05089 SAO PAULO 10. Tel. 261.1920
a Senador Dantas 19 s/205-6, RIO DE JANEIRO GB.
. 232.07.32

NADA
rouf Publishing Company Limited,
82 St. Catherine Street West,
CNTRÉAL, Que. H3H 1M7. Tel. (514)937.3519
TAWA, Ont. K1P 5A6, 61 Sparks Street

NMARK – DANEMARK
inksgaard Export and Subscription Service
, Nørre Søgade
C 1370 KØBENHAVN K. Tel. +45.1.12.85.70

NLAND – FINLANDE
ateeminen Kirjakauppa
skuskatu 1, 00100 HELSINKI 10. Tel. 65.11.22

ANCE
reau des Publications de l'OCDE,
ue André-Pascal, 75775 PARIS CEDEX 16. Tel. (1) 524.81.67
incipal correspondant :
602 AIX-EN-PROVENCE : Librairie de l'Université.
. 26.18.08

RMANY – ALLEMAGNE
CD Publications and Information Center
Smrockstrasse 5300 BONN Tel. (0228) 21.60.45

REECE – GRÈCE
rairie Kauffmann, 28 rue du Stade,
HÈNES 132. Tel. 322.21.60

NG-KONG
vernment Information Services,
blications/Sales Section, Baskerville House,
F., 22 Ice House Street

ELAND – ISLANDE
aebjörn Jónsson and Co., h.f.,
tinarstraeti 4 and 9, P.O.B. 1131, REYKJAVIK.
1 13133/14281/11936

DIA – INDE
xford Book and Stationery Co. :
EW DELHI-1, Scindia House. Tel. 45896
ALCUTTA 700016, 17 Park Street. Tel. 240832

DONESIA – INDONÉSIE
DIN-LIPI, P.O. Box 3065/JKT., JAKARTA, Tel. 583467

ELAND – IRLANDE
OC Publishers – Library Suppliers
North Frederick Street, DUBLIN 1 Tel. 744835-749677

ALY – ITALIE
breria Commissionaria Sansoni :
a Lamarmora 45, 50121 FIRENZE. Tel. 579751
a Bartolini 29, 20155 MILANO. Tel. 365083
b-depositari :
itrice e Libreria Herder,
azza Montecitorio 120, 00 186 ROMA. Tel. 6794628
breria Hoepli, Via Hoepli 5, 20121 MILANO. Tel. 865446
breria Lattes, Via Garibaldi 3, 10122 TORINO. Tel. 519274
a diffusione delle edizioni OCSE è inoltre assicurata dalle migliori
erie nelle città più importanti.

PAN – JAPON
ECD Publications and Information Center,
adic Akasaka Bldg., 2-3-4 Akasaka,
inato-ku, TOKYO 107 Tel. 586.2016

OREA – CORÉE
an Korea Book Corporation,
O. Box n° 101 Kwangwhamun, SÉOUL. Tel. 72.7369

LEBANON – LIBAN
Documenta Scientifica/Redico,
Edison Bu Iding, Bliss Street, P.O. Box 5641, BEIRUT.
Tel. 354425 – 344425

MALAYSIA – MALAISIE
and/et SINGAPORE - SINGAPOUR
University of Malaysia Co-operative Bookshop Ltd.
P.O. Box 27, Jalan Pantai Baru
KUALA LUMPUR. Tel. 51425, 54058, 54361

THE NETHERLANDS – PAYS-BAS
Staatsuitgeverij
Verzendboekhandel Chr. Plantijnstraat 1
Postbus 20014
2500 EA S-GRAVENAGE. Tel. nr. 070.789911
Voor bestel ingen: Tel. 070.789208

NEW ZEALAND – NOUVELLE-ZÉLANDE
Publications Section,
Governme t Printing Office Bookshops:
AUCKLAND: Retail Bookshop: 25 Rutland Street,
Mail Orders: 85 Beach Road, Private Bag C.P.O.
HAMILTON: Retail Ward Street,
Mail Orders, P.O. Box 857
WELLINGTON: Retail: Mulgrave Street (Head Office),
Cubacade World Trade Centre
Mail Orders: Private Bag
CHRISTCHURCH: Retail: 159 Hereford Street,
Mail Orders: Private Bag
DUNEDIN: Retail: Princes Street
Mail Order P.O. Box 1104

NORWAY – NORVÈGE
J.G. TANUM A/S Karl Johansgate 43
P.O. Box 77 Sentrum OSLO 1. Tel. (02) 80.12.60

PAKISTAN
Mirza Book Agency, 65 Shahrah Quaid-E-Azam, LAHORE 3.
Tel. 66839

PHILIPPINES
National Book Store, Inc.
Library Services Division, P.O. Box 1934, MANILA.
Tel. Nos. 49.43.06 to 09, 40.53.45, 49.45.12

PORTUGAL
Livraria Portugal, Rua do Carmo 70-74,
1117 LISBOA CODEX. Tel. 360582/3

SPAIN – ESPAGNE
Mundi-Prensa Libros, S.A.
Castelló 37 Apartado 1223, MADRID-1. Tel. 275.46.55
Libreria Bastinos, Pelayo 52, BARCELONA 1. Tel. 222.06.00

SWEDEN – SUÈDE
AB CE Fritzes Kungl Hovbokhandel,
Box 16 355 S 103 27 STH, Regeringsgatan 12,
DS STOCKHOLM. Tel. 08/23.89.00

SWITZERLAND – SUISSE
OECD Publications and Information Center
4 Simrocks rasse 5300 BONN. Tel. (0228) 21.60.45
Local Agents/Agents locaux
Librairie Payot, 6 rue Grenus, 1211 GENÈVE 11. Tel. 022.31.89.50
Freihofer A.G., Weinbergstr. 109, CH-8006 ZÜRICH.
Tel. 01.363.4282

THAILAND – THAILANDE
Suksit Siam Co., Ltd., 1715 Rama IV Rd,
Samyan, BANGKOK 5. Tel. 2511630

TURKEY – TURQUIE
Kültur Yayinlari Is-Türk Ltd. Sti.
Atatürk Bulvari No : 77/B
KIZILAY ANKARA. Tel. 17 02 66
Dolmabahce Cad. No : 29
BESIKTAS/ISTANBUL. Tel. 60 71 88

UNITED KINGDOM – ROYAUME-UNI
H.M. Stationery Office, P.O.B. 569,
LONDON SE1 9NH. Tel. 01.928.6977, Ext. 410 or
49 High Holborn, LONDON WC1V 6 HB (personal callers)
Branches at: EDINBURGH, BIRMINGHAM, BRISTOL,
MANCHESTER, CARDIFF, BELFAST.

UNITED STATES OF AMERICA – ÉTATS-UNIS
OECD Publications and Information Center, Suite 1207,
1750 Pennsylvania Ave., N.W. WASHINGTON, D.C.20006 – 4582
Tel. (202) 724.1857

VENEZUELA
Libreria del Este, Avda. F. Miranda 52, Edificio Galipan,
CARACAS 106. Tel. 32.23.01/33.26.04/33.24.73

YUGOSLAVIA – YOUGOSLAVIE
Jugoslovenska Knjiga, Terazije 27, P.O.B. 36, BEOGRAD.
Tel. 621.992

Les commandes provenant de pays où l'OCDE n'a pas encore désigné de dépositaire peuvent être adressées à :
OCDE, Bureau des Publications, 2, rue André-Pascal, 75775 PARIS CEDEX 16.

Orders and inquiries from countries where sales agents have not yet been appointed may be sent to:
OECD, Publications Office, 2 rue André-Pascal, 75775 PARIS CEDEX 16.

OECD PUBLICATIONS, 2, rue André-Pascal, 75775 PARIS CEDEX 16 - No. 42153 1982
PRINTED IN FRANCE
(21 82 02 1) ISBN 92-64-12292-3